BOOZE
AND THE
BADGE

A COP'S BATTLE WITH THE BOTTLE

BARRY RUHL
SGT. (RET.) ONTARIO PROVINCIAL POLICE
WITH DAVID HOATH, PhD

FriesenPress

Suite 300 - 990 Fort St
Victoria, BC, V8V 3K2
Canada

www.friesenpress.com

Copyright © 2020 by Barry Ruhl
First Edition — 2020
David Hoath, PhD – Editor

All rights reserved.

No part of this publication may be reproduced in any form, or by any means, electronic or mechanical, including photocopying, recording, or any information browsing, storage, or retrieval system, without permission in writing from FriesenPress.

ISBN
978-1-5255-8532-6 (Hardcover)
978-1-5255-8533-3 (Paperback)
978-1-5255-8534-0 (eBook)

1. BIO027000 Biography & Autobiography, Law Enforcement

Distributed to the trade by The Ingram Book Company

This book is dedicated to Pat, my soulmate.
You have been forgiving and supportive throughout my intemperate journey.
Together forever.

I also dedicate this book to my brothers and sisters in blue.
Recovery defines the person riding on the waves of sobriety.

CONTENTS

ACKNOWLEDGEMENTS..VII
INTRODUCTION..IX

PART ONE: BOOZE BEFORE: THE BADGE
CHAPTER 1: SCHOOL'S OUT...1

PART TWO: BOOZE WITH: THE BADGE
CHAPTER 2: SUITING UP AND: SHIPPING OUT................... 19
CHAPTER 3: EXPO 67..37
CHAPTER 4: KITCHENER:: 1967–1980..............................47
CHAPTER 5: SOBRIETY AND THE ROAD TO RECOVERY..........69
CHAPTER 6: THE BARRIE: DISTRICT CRIME UNIT................. 81
CHAPTER 7: BARRIE DETACHMENT................................105

PART 3: BOOZE AFTER: THE BADGE
CHAPTER 8: ADDICTION: COUNSELLOR............................125
CHAPTER 9: YOU HAVE: PROSTATE CANCER......................133
CHAPTER 10: WASTED DAYS AND WASTED NIGHTS............ 141
CHAPTER 11: SNOWBIRDS...147
EPILOGUE: A WIFE'S: PERSPECTIVE 157

ACKNOWLEDGEMENTS

This book would not have been possible without the assistance of Dr. David Hoath.

I also want to offer my sincere thanks to our son, Jeff, for his support, encouragement, and advice. Proud parents indeed.

INTRODUCTION

Booze, and the Badge describes the roller coaster ride I was on for over sixty years with a very seductive and dangerous companion-alcohol.

I had my first drink when I was fifteen and my last drink when I was seventy. A drunken "crash" was the motivation that caused me to finally seek sobriety. I was staggering home from a party, lost my balance, and fell ass over tea kettle. For several hours I was immobile and scared shit-less. That was the "last call." I'm sober now and living one day at a time.

I have deconstructed my life's journey to better understand myself and my alcoholism. For much of my life, I played the game of saying I was an alcoholic but not really believing it. So, every time I took a drink, I believed I was in control. Nevertheless, every time I did, it was proof positive I was an alcoholic. Consequently, I surrendered to "Little Barry's" entreaties and proved just how vulnerable I was.

Who is "Little Barry?" A part of me that's impulsive, reckless, blind to consequences, and very, very persuasive. The part of me that likes to get his own way no matter what. A small voice inside my head that seeks uninhibited "pleasure" by getting drunk. When I was drinking, he could con me to act out. He's a master at manipulation until I acquiesce. Little Barry is narcissistic and demands recognition and admiration. Little Barry is dangerous. I permitted him to do things that, were it not for the grace of God, could have had catastrophic outcomes. I embarked on many failed attempts to learn how to manage Little Barry, and I'll never let my guard down because he's always waiting in the wings when I'm mad, glad, or sad.

Alcoholism is a malady as invisible as air and as insidious as cancer. In the beginning, drinking is essentially a social lubricant. However, in time it becomes prominent in an alcoholic's life. In many situations, it can lead to adverse socio-economic consequences, including marital discord, workplace conflict, financial stress, legal issues, and health concerns. I worked alongside hundreds of men and women during my thirty years of serving in OPP "blue"[1] and I know how ubiquitous and pernicious booze is in cop culture.

Why did I write this book? Initially, I wanted to give my police family a heads-up because they could become entangled in this self-destructive "life trap."[2] I also hope officers struggling with substance abuse understand there's light at the end of that very dark tunnel. So, *Booze and the Badge*, is dedicated to my brothers and sisters *in law*. It may sound cliché, but even if one officer is motivated to seek sobriety, then the decision to bare my soul will be have been worth it. There has also been a therapeutic benefit from writing *Booze and the Badge*. I know myself a little better, especially Little Barry.

Finally, I wrote *Booze and the Badge* for Pat, my dear wife. She has been my soulmate for nearly fifty years and has remained at my side despite the stupid, selfish, and disastrous choices I have made. Together forever.

---

1   Slang term for police or police uniform

2   This term is borrowed from Jeffrey E. Young and Janet S. Klosko's book, *Reinventing Your Life*. (New York: Penguin Books 1994).

PART ONE
BOOZE BEFORE THE BADGE

CHAPTER 1
SCHOOL'S OUT

School's out forever
School's out for summer
School's out with fever
School's out completely

– Alice Cooper

ALICE COOPER'S "SCHOOL'S OUT," COULD have been my swan song. The morning I was to write the grade twelve compulsory departmental exam, I arrived late and hungover. Upon reflection, celebrating my nineteenth birthday on a school night was stupid. However, when booze was involved, self-destructive decisions were never far away. It didn't help that I wasn't academically inclined. I failed grade nine, passed grade ten, failed grade eleven, and enrolled in the special commercial program the following year. My saving grace was my athletic prowess. I was a key player on the basketball teams that won both the Junior and Senior Western Ontario Secondary School Association (OFSSA) "A" championships. I also topped the field in the senior track and field championship, running barefoot and puffing on a cigarette between events.

When I entered the classroom, I was greeted by an agitated nun, Sister Gerrarda. "You're late!" she exclaimed. She was an incredible teacher. She cared for her students and had a reputation for finding them steady employment. I wasn't going to be one of those students. Rather, by the tone of her voice and body language, I knew I was in trouble—big trouble!

"You won't be writing the exam, and I suggest you go home!" she said. I tried to offer a plausible explanation, but my pleas fell on deaf ears. I left St. Joseph's High for the last time. Walking home, I felt physically and emotionally drained, thinking the boozing had finally caught up with me. Although the hangover would subside, the feelings of shame and rejection would linger for a long time.

When I arrived home, I told my parents I had been expelled, but they didn't appear to be too concerned. There was never an expectation that my siblings and me would excel in school. Nonetheless, my brother Doug graduated from Fanshawe College, my brother Phil graduated from the University of Waterloo, and despite my early failures in school, I obtained a bachelor's degree in sociology from the University of Waterloo and a bachelor's degree in social work from York University.

PARTY CENTRAL

I was raised in Lynhurst on the outskirts of St. Thomas, Ontario. My father, Nelson "Red" Ruhl, enjoyed drinking a lot. Dad was a well-known musician (saxophone) and proprietor of a furniture store. Often, there was a steady flow of hangers-on visiting dad, including politicians, businessmen, and musicians. Furthermore, the expansive acreage behind our home was the ideal venue for socializing. I recall a lawyer, an alderman, and the owner of the local ambulance service arriving on our doorstep, booze in hand. It didn't matter what Dad was doing; he was in!

I believe these frequent visits took a toll on my mother, who seldom drank and suffered in silence. So, I never knew what she was thinking and can only guess that Dad's excessive drinking adversely affected her. Perhaps the fact that her father, Leo Whitty, was an alcoholic conjured up unpleasant memories for her.

I wasn't concerned when Dad entertained at home, but it bothered me when "the bar was open" at N. J. Ruhl Furniture. I recall one boozehound who visited the store daily. Dad and his "buddy" drank and played cribbage for hours. Although I knew drinking at the business wasn't appropriate, I also knew my advice wouldn't be well received. Unfortunately, a few years after the store opened, Westinghouse issued a demand note, and Dad filed for bankruptcy.

My father passed peacefully in 1972. He was sixty-one. The official cause of death was congestive heart failure, but the many years he drank, and the stress precipitated by the bankruptcy contributed significantly to his early demise.

My father, Nelson "Red" Ruhl (Credit: Barry Ruhl)

I have heard it said you can tell how a person was liked by the number of people at their funeral. If this is a measure of affection, Nelson "Red" Ruhl was very well liked, as evidenced by the large gathering. I can still picture the plethora of floral tributes that adorned the parlor, including an arrangement of his beloved saxophone. He touched many people in a positive way, and I'm proud of my father. Nevertheless, he was taken too soon.

As an aside, I was excited to learn that his music lives on. A friend from St. Thomas had an audio recording of dad's band playing at the local Legion hall. I obtained a copy and imagine the rush of hearing him play years later. I feel truly blessed to have this everlasting keepsake.

NATURE, NURTURE, OR BOTH?

When I revisit my formative years in terms of what I learned as an addiction counsellor, I wonder why booze has had such a deleterious effect on my life. My studies indicate there are two theories, in terms of addiction: nature versus nurture. So, was I genetically predisposed to alcoholism, or was it learned behaviour? Or was it both? I recall watching Dad and his friends drinking and thinking that was the way to have fun. However, the bankruptcy also played a factor in my proclivity to drink because I felt embarrassed when I was with my friends. In the good old days, bankruptcy and failure had a symbiotic relationship. Consequently, I drank in part to numb the shame.

CHASING THE HIGH

I was fifteen when I drank my first beer, although Dad gave me an occasional sip before that. I snuck a bottle of beer from the cold cellar and went for a walk in Lynhurst. When the coast was clear, I uncapped the bottle, took a few sips, and a warm sensation coursed through my body. It wasn't long before I was chasing that high. I drank almost every weekend. In fact, the weekends were no longer enjoyable if I wasn't drinking. It seemed I needed booze to enjoy myself, and it wasn't long before I was binge drinking.[3] On the weekends, I cruised the backroads in Elgin County sipping beer with my buddies, listening to rock 'n' roll, and checking the rear view mirror for the "black-and-whites." When the beer was gone, we joined our friends at the local high schools or arena for dances. I really enjoyed dancing and was quite proficient at it, even winning a few competitions. Eventually, six beers didn't do it for me. So, I began chasing beer with shots of liquor. Party on! My excessive drinking led to a myriad of high-risk behaviours, including driving while impaired, passing out with the car running, and choking on a sandwich. I also had my first encounter with the police while driving impaired.

On a late summer evening, I was returning home in my 1950 Ford after last call at the iconic Royal Hotel in St. Thomas. My father had recently purchased the car for me for the grand sum of $100. Though I had to wire the driver's door shut, I was proud of my first set of wheels. So, with the temperamental door firmly wired shut, I set off to show my wheels to my buddies at the hotel.

When I arrived, I parked on Talbot Street and entered the "Men Only" entrance."[4] Every time I entered that smoke-filled room and smelled the odor of stale beer and heard the sound of clattering shuffleboard rocks, I felt a sense of anticipation and excitement. When I told my buddies about my new wheels, they rushed out to see it. I was the brunt of more than a few jokes, when they saw that the driver's door was wired shut. Someone even referred to me as "Kamikaze."

I drank and played shuffleboard until last call. Even though I was three sheets to the wind, I managed to win enough games to pay for my drinks. Bonus! After last call, I bid my

---

[3] The National Institute on Alcohol Abuse and Alcoholism (NIAAA) defines binge drinking as "a pattern of drinking that brings a person's blood alcohol concentration (BAC) to 0.08 grams of alcohol per decilitre (0.08 g/dL or 100 mL of blood). This typically happens when men consume 5 or more drinks, and when women consume 4 or more drinks in about 2 hours."

[4] In those days, there were two entrances to hotels, an entrance for men and a "Ladies and Escorts Entrance."

buddies goodnight and left the hotel, pissed. Nevertheless, I managed to rev up the Ford and head home, never thinking that I might be stopped by the police. Wrong! When I was about a quarter mile from home, I spotted the ominous flashing lights of an OPP cruiser in the rear-view mirror. *Shit! Now, I'm in BIG trouble*, I thought. As the officer approached, I tried to appear sober. I lowered my window and looked at the officer as he shone his flashlight inside the car.

"Good evening," he said. "I stopped you because your taillights are out. Can I see your driver's licence, registration, and insurance?" That was going to be a problem because I was only eighteen, and the drinking age in Ontario in 1962 was twenty-one.

"Sorry, Officer, I don't have my licence with me," I replied. "It's at home."

"Have you been drinking?" he asked.

"Yes, sir. I had a couple of beers at the Royal." Of course, then he wanted to know how old I was. When I advised him. I was twenty-one, he wanted to know where I was going. "Home," I replied.

The officer tried to open the driver's door. "It's wired shut, Officer," I said. I could see I was testing his patience. He looked the car over, and I wondered if he was going to have it towed. But then I had something else to worry about: he wanted to follow me home to check my driver's licence!

My mind raced to think of an excuse for lying as we neared my residence, but nothing came to mind. The jig was up.

When we arrived at my residence, I approached him. "Sorry, Officer," I said. "I lied. I actually have my licence on me, and I'm only eighteen."

"It's not smart to lie to the police," he said, stating the obvious. He also said I could be charged with drinking underage and obstructing justice (which was a Criminal Code offence.) He didn't mention impaired driving, and I knew I would blow over .08. Nevertheless, he gave me a break and only charged me with not having taillights. I was so relieved that I almost hugged him.

"Sorry for lying, and thank you for giving me a break," I muttered.

Most people would consider this an important lesson. Not me. I continued to push my luck for many years. You see, Little Barry didn't learn from that initial encounter with the police. He tended to make the same mistake repeatedly, even though the handwriting was on the wall. My drinking was out of control, and I was a burgeoning alcoholic.

The consequences hit home when I watched my classmates enter Holy Angel's Church to receive their graduation diplomas, and I realized the mess I had made of my life. Fear and panic gripped me as I pondered my future. *Where will I find work?* I wondered. *What company will hire a dropout or, in my case, a "kick out?"* I was also crushed by the reality that even if I obtained employment, it would likely be a dead-end job.

TAKING CARE OF BUSINESS

I eventually found work at a frozen food plant in London. My job consisted of selecting produce from a freezer and taking the items to the customers' vehicles. For my labour, I received one dollar an hour and no benefits. However, there was one perk. On Friday afternoons, the boss treated me and my co-worker, Joe Irons, to mouth-watering corned beef sandwiches and scrumptious kosher pickles. Fridays were always a highlight in an otherwise unchallenging job. However, there was one Friday when the luncheon wasn't enjoyable!

We were eating with a company salesman, and I happened to mention I was looking for other employment. Without missing a beat, he said, "Forget it, pal. This is the only job you'll ever have!" I was dumbfounded and pissed- off.

"You're wrong," I said. "I'll get a better job!" Undeterred, he continued asserting that I was destined for dead-end work. This loudmouth proffered an opinion, even though he knew nothing about me. Despite my protests, his pessimistic prediction caused me to consider my future. *Is he right? Will I ever get a better job? Will I ever amount to anything?*

I detested working at the store, and I lived solely for the weekends when I frequented my three favorite haunts: The Brass Rail, the CPR Hotel (nicknamed "Ceeps"), and the Latin Quarter. My life pretty much personified Freddy Fender's song, "Wasted Days and Wasted Nights." I trolled the bars, discreetly knocking back vodka or rye from a mickey[5] that I stashed in my pocket. I enjoyed the sexy go-go dancers at the Brass Rail, especially when Rompin' Ronnie Hawkins was performing. As the evening progressed, the go-go dancers got sexier, and Ronnie's music got "rompier." Party on!

However, the mornings after were a much different story. The fun-filled barhopping was inevitably replaced by the dreaded hangover. Nevertheless, after I downed a few beers,

---

5   A 375-ml bottle of liquor.

otherwise known as the "hair of the dog,"[6] I was good to go. Unfortunately, the weekends ended too soon, and with the arrival of "Blue Monday," I was back at my dead-end job. It seemed the pessimistic pronouncement from the bombastic salesman might become a reality.

Then a glimmer of hope sprang up when I spoke to an officer with the London Police Department (LPD). He was enquiring about a product and, out of the blue, asked if I ever considered becoming a police officer. Surprisingly, I had never thought of becoming a cop, even though my mother's brother, Jack Whitty, was the assistant commissioner of the Ontario Provincial Police (OPP). I had always admired Uncle Jack, and it seemed like an opportune time to consider the prospect.

Over the next few weeks, I weighed the pros and cons. On one hand, law enforcement would be a rewarding career, an occupation where I could serve the public and chase the bad guys. On the other hand, it was essentially paramilitary. I was also concerned that "wearing the blue" would put a damper on my drinking. Nevertheless, after balancing the pros and cons, I decided to test the waters and apply. I reasoned if it wasn't for me, I'd simply quit. I completed the application, and within a couple of weeks received a letter directing me to report to the recruitment unit on July 6 at 10 a.m.

I was quite nervous entering the fortress-like headquarters at 14 King Street. I met the recruitment coordinator, who introduced me to Chief Findlay Carroll. We shook hands and spoke briefly, then he nodded to my escort, and we left. I assume the chief's nod meant I could continue in the process.

A few days later, I was interviewed by a personnel officer. During the interview, he asked why I wanted to be a cop. I replied that I thought serving the public would be rewarding, and he nodded, perhaps signifying that was a good answer. I had a sense that the interviewer was pleased with my performance, but his last question sealed my fate with the London Police Service. He asked me the name of the astronaut who had just orbited the earth.[7]

"I don't know," I said.

"My six-year-old daughter could answer that question," he replied in surprise.

---

6   An alcoholic beverage consumed as a hangover remedy. The phrase comes from the expression "hair of the dog that bit you," meaning that the best cure for what ails you is to have some more of it.

7   John Glenn Jr. on February 20, 1962.

"Well your six-year-old daughter isn't applying for this job!" I said without thinking. If I had listened carefully, I think I would have been able to hear the *gong* because the interview ended shortly after that exchange. A few days later, I received a letter from the LPD thanking me for my interest, but I was no longer being considered.

SELF-REFLECTION

Clearly, I wasn't thinking when I offered that flippant, hair-trigger response to the officer's remark. I wonder what caused me to lash out at such an inopportune time. I was trying to secure a job, a career, for the rest of my life, and I blew off the interviewer with an impulsive, thoughtless response. What the hell was I thinking? One answer to this question came to me after I joined the OPP. In 1979, Dr. John Sawatsky, OPP psychologist, wrote of my personality,

> He has a high degree of self-confidence, and is inclined to be strongly assertive, and forthright. He has a positive attitude about people and although he is rather "dominant," or at least, forthright with people, he prefers co-operation and teamwork…he is inclined to be stable and not subject to pressures and stresses and able to maintain optimism.

I have since learned through experience that my "assertive dominance" can be triggered whenever I feel put down or ridiculed. As I indicated earlier, I don't take orders well, and I don't submit readily to others who attempt to dominate or control me. In this case, I understand that when the interviewer compared me to his six-year-old daughter, Little Barry felt he was denigrating my intelligence and putting me down. But he may have merely been testing my temperament to see how I would respond. My immediate reaction in that instance was to lash out, and it cost me the possibility of becoming a cop. It wouldn't be the last time Little Barry led me to self-defeating behaviour.

A few months passed, and I was still trapped in the dead-end job and frequenting my favorite haunts. One evening, I was pondering my future over a few drinks at the Brass Rail when I met a former classmate from St. Joseph's who worked for the Canadian National Railway (CNR). He told me the company was hiring and suggested I apply.

I was hired right away and given the task of filing freight bills, which felt like another dead-end job. However, being an eternal optimist, I realized the CNR might have other employment opportunities.

BOOZING AT THE BEND

Tripping to Grand Bend was a rite of passage for teenagers from Southwestern Ontario. "The Bend" is on the eastern shores of pristine Lake Huron. Naturally, when I turned nineteen, it was time for me and my three buddies to check it out.

In preparation, I managed to persuade my Aunt Jane (my mother's sister) to buy us a case of beer. Then we hopped into my 1951 Nash,[8] anticipating a weekend of fun in the sun: booze, sex, and rock 'n' roll. Tripping to the Bend was a blast for four testosterone-driven buddies listening to rock 'n' roll and babbling about getting lucky!

When we arrived, we cruised the busy main strip and noticed the ominous outlaw bikers wearing their "colours" or "patches, but the plethora of bikinis was much more appealing! Party! But first things first.

After getting our bearings, we rented a dilapidated cottage at an exorbitant cost. Next, we started to drink. After hours of drinking and partying, I passed out on the beach. I was awakened by a friendly police officer who suggested I move on, which I didn't do. I passed out again and was awakened a second time by some not-so-friendly party animals who proceeded to throw me into frigid Lake Huron. To add insult to injury, a pair of brand-new desert boots "walked away," never to be seen again. But that wasn't as bad as my buddy, who pissed off a biker and was punched out!

The next morning, our intrepid troop headed home with our tails between our legs. We were hungover, and contrary to expectations, no one got lucky. Furthermore, I lost a new pair of boots, and my buddy who was whacked looked like he had run into a wall. Inasmuch as the weekend was a downer, one might think it would have been a wake-up call. Nope! We continued to frequent the Bend, searching for the elusive Lady Luck.

SELF-REFLECTION

When I recall drinking at the Imperial Hotel at the Bend, George Thorogood's songs, "One Bourbon, One Scotch, One Beer" and "I Drink Alone" could have been written for me. Although I didn't consider myself an alcoholic, I know that my preference for drinking alone is a characteristic of alcoholism.[9] Unfortunately, the salesman's prediction that

---

8   Incidentally, I dragged the Nash at the Sparta Drag Strip, detailing my wheels with "The Green Pig" and "Tuned by Bugs Bunny." It blazed through the quarter mile at an impressive forty seconds flat!

9   21 Warning Signs of Alcoholism: https://www.quitalcohol.com/21-warning-signs-of-alcoholism.html.

I wouldn't amount to anything bothered me to the extent that when I returned from the Bend, I called my Uncle Jack, hoping he could help me decide if I was made of the "right stuff" to become an OPP officer. Furthermore, even though I didn't realize it at the time, Jack and I were stricken with the same malady. We were both alcoholics.

MEETING UNCLE JACK

I called Uncle Jack to arrange a meeting. I had considered meeting at OPP headquarters because I wanted him to be sober. Nevertheless, I decided to meet at his house in an informal setting. Although there were occasions when Jack got drunk and retired early, there were other times when we talked into the night when he was sober.

Thankfully, Jack was sober when he greeted me. I explained I was unhappy at the CNR and wondered what his thoughts were about my applying to the OPP. He asked why I wanted to become a police officer. I said I thought it would be a rewarding career and an occupation where I could help people. Jack nodded as though he agreed. However, he also discussed the social isolation that officers encountered on the job.

"Keep in mind, Barry, when your friends are socializing, you may be working afternoons or nights. Eventually, you'll be spending a great deal of time with your shift." He was quiet for a moment, and then he shared some of his investigations, including violent crimes, horrific motor vehicle collisions, and heart-wrenching tragedies involving children. As he reminisced, I pictured myself in those situations. Did I have the right stuff?

I asked Jack why he became a cop. He said that initially, he was attracted to the decent pay and benefits. "For me it was really about helping people, and to this day, I still recall with satisfaction the folks I helped," he added. Then he paused. "I think you should consider applying, Barry."

After a couple of weeks of deliberation, I sent in my application. Six months later, I received notification to appear before the Civil Service Board (CSB).

My uncle, Assistant Commissioner Jack Whitty
(Credit: Barry Ruhl)

DYING TO JOIN THE OPP

I suspect there are times in everyone's life when they do something that defies any logic or rationale. For some reason, I tend to do that a lot.

My interview with the CSB was scheduled for a Monday morning. However, on the Sunday prior to my interview, I was walking along Wellington Road in London with orange-coloured hair and being greeted with honking horns and catcalls. Self-conscious, I quickened my pace, and by the time I arrived at my girlfriend's house, I was in a panic thinking that being interviewed with orange hair would be a game stopper!

By way of explanation, let me offer a flashback to the previous evening. My buddy and I took our girlfriends to the drive-in to see *How the West Was Won*. Of course, a quantity of booze was consumed during the evening, and for some reason that escapes me, I agreed to have my hair treated with hydrogen peroxide. I awoke the next morning, hungover and bleary eyed. I stumbled into the bathroom and looked in the mirror.

Holy Christ! My hair is orange! I thought I was going to puke. *What if my hair is ruined? Why did I allow them to dye my hair? How can I appear before the board looking like this? What the hell is the matter with me? Why would I get drunk and jeopardize, the interview?* This wasn't the first time I screwed up. I recall how ashamed I felt when I was expelled from St.

Joseph's High, and here I was on the precipice of doing the same thing. What the hell was wrong with me?

In desperation, I called my girlfriend, and she instructed me to purchase chestnut-coloured hair dye. When I entered the pharmacy, I felt like a kid buying "safes" for the first time. I asked the clerk for the location of their hair dye. With a slight smirk, she glanced at my hair and then directed me to the appropriate aisle. With dye in hand and downcast eyes, I quickly left the store.

When I arrived at my girlfriend's, she greeted me with an impish smile. Then she applied the dye and vigorously rubbed it into my scalp. Thankfully, my hair returned to a more natural colour, and I chilled out despite the lingering hangover.

When I rolled out of bed on the morning of the interview, I rushed to the mirror, prompted by the fear that my hair had reverted to flaming orange. When I was assured it was the original colour, I readied myself for the interview. I recalled Uncle Jack's advice: "Make sure your suit is clean, your pants pressed, and your shoes shined. Remember, stand erect, appear calm, and think before you speak."

I was quite anxious when I appeared before the three-member board. The first question they asked was, "Why do you want to become a police officer?" I recalled my conversation with Jack and replied that I wanted to become an officer because I wanted to help people. That response seemed to satisfy them. A few other questions stumped me, and I simply said, "I'm sorry, but I don't know the answer." When the interview concluded, I felt ambivalent. On one hand, I thought I had given comprehensive answers to most of their questions, but the few questions I couldn't answer nagged at me.

Months passed, and I didn't hear anything. I was beginning to think I hadn't been successful, so I called Jack. He said I needed to be patient. He was right. A week later I received a letter confirming that I could continue the application process.

The following month, I wrote an exam at a high school in London. It included multiple-choice questions and an essay. The essay was a composition on what the maple leaf flag meant to me. I finished the exam early and then left.

Approximately a month later, I was notified that I had passed the exam and was required to complete the final two steps in the selection process: a medical examination and a background check. It was at that point that I finally allowed myself to believe I would soon be driving a black-and-white. Then calamity struck!

Shortly after receiving the notification, I was involved in a head-on collision in St. Thomas. As you might guess, I was barhopping with a buddy, Steve Auld,[10*] on a Saturday evening. We had visited several bars and were heading to another when Steve, who was drunk, grabbed the steering wheel, causing me to lose control. The car veered wildly, struck a curb, careened across the road, and hit an oncoming car head-on. The impact tore the hood right off my Austin Healey Sprite. Fortunately, no one was seriously injured.

After the dust settled, and I regained my composure, I figured Steve was in trouble for grabbing the wheel. So, with no thought of the unintended consequences, I decided to cover for him. When the investigating officer asked me what happened, I told him I was lighting a cigarette when the car hit the curb and crossed the road, striking the other vehicle. In my mind, I thought my story would absolve both of us. The officer wrote the statement down and read it back to me. "Is that what happened?" he asked. I agreed and signed the statement. I was gobsmacked when he issued me a ticket for careless driving, a relatively serious Highway Traffic Act violation. Now, I was angry at my drunken buddy. I was also upset with myself. Out of some silly sense of loyalty to a transient "friend," I had just jeopardized my entire future.

SELF-REFLECTION

I'm sure you've noticed a pattern by now. I've admitted to being impulsive, but it seems that I was allowing Little Barry's impulsiveness and my behaviour to govern my actions at the worst-possible times. I had just received notification that I had been accepted in the next stage of the OPP selection process. My future was looking very promising. Then my buddy dumped me in a pile of shit and what did I do? I threw myself under the proverbial bus. Why? Just so Little Barry could be "that guy," the guy who covered for his buddy.

Although it took me a long time to realize it, I know now that Little Barry is quite narcissistic. He likes to be the centre of attention, the "man," the guy who people admire, and who better to admire than a "stand-up guy" who protects his buddies? I didn't think I would get in trouble because I only looked at the situation from my own perspective. Although ostensibly, I was doing my buddy a favour, Little Barry saw an opportunity to be the "big man on campus," to be the "star," and it backfired big time.

---

10   *Whenever an asterisk is used, it indicates a name has been changed.

On the day I was to be interviewed by the OPP, I wondered what would happen when the OPP heard about the careless driving charge. A staff superintendent (s/supt.) arrived and, following some chitchat, he asked me a series of questions pertaining to my credit rating, marital status, and interests. Whew, he didn't mention offences. Then the other shoe dropped.

"OK, Barry, I've checked the database, and you don't have a criminal record. What about offenses under the Highway Traffic or Liquor Control acts?"

I paused for a few seconds, trying to remain calm, then cleared my throat. "Well, I was recently involved in an accident and charged with careless driving."

He noted my reply. "Well, in view of the charge, your application will be placed on hold pending the outcome."

After he left, I reflected on my predicament. If convicted, I could kiss a career with the OPP goodbye. I couldn't let that happen.

I hired a lawyer, and he advised that if Steve didn't testify, I'd probably be convicted. Luckily, I managed to contact Steve, and after explaining my predicament, he agreed to testify.

On the day of the trial, I entered the courtroom and immediately recognized the magistrate. Fred Barnum had attended the basketball games at St. Joseph's High when I played for the senior team. I wondered if that was a good omen or a sign of impending disaster. Next, I noticed the OPP staff superintendent in the front row with his notebook open. *Shit* I thought, *this really could be a disaster.*

When my case was called, I entered a plea of not guilty. The investigating officer provided the court with the facts, including the rationale for charging me with careless driving. My attorney asked the officer if the passenger in my vehicle was present in the courtroom, and he pointed to him. I was next to testify. I knew my future with the OPP was on the line, and everything depended on Steve's testimony.

My lawyer led me through the circumstances involving the collision. I explained that Steve had grabbed the steering wheel, causing me to lose control, and I had lied to the officer because I wanted to protect my friend. My lawyer inquired about my future aspirations. I testified that I had applied to become a member of the OPP and was in the latter stages of the selection process. When I completed my testimony, it was time for Steve to tell the truth!

He appeared nervous as he took the stand. Nevertheless, he admitted to what he had done. On cross-examination, the crown attorney asked why he had grabbed the steering wheel. Although Steve couldn't recall why he grabbed the wheel, he admitted that it was a stupid thing to do and said he was sorry. The case was now before the court.

In view of Steve's inculpatory testimony, the careless driving charge was dismissed. Whew! You can't imagine how relieved I felt when Magistrate Barnum pronounced a verdict of "not guilty." I was ecstatic! But that was short lived when I was confronted by the angry investigating officer, who was noticeably agitated, "I've got news for you, Ruhl. You'll never get in the OPP because I'm charging you with public mischief." My stomach sank, my heart jumped to my throat, and my mind raced. *Public mischief, what the hell is that?*

When I left the courthouse, I was reeling in a chaotic maelstrom of fear and uncertainty. What the hell was I going to do? You guessed it. I spent the remainder of the day in the Royal Hotel, getting drunk and ruminating about the cop's threat.

For several weeks I wondered if the officer was going to follow through with it. As time passed and nothing happened, I realized he was probably just blowing off steam. Ultimately, no charges were forthcoming, and I felt that my window of "OPPortunity" was ready for me to enter.

But I was still waiting for correspondence from the OPP and was concerned that the careless driving charge might have sealed my fate with the organization. After all, I had lied to the investigating officer. Nevertheless, on June 4, 1964, just as I was ready to throw in the towel, I received a letter from the OPP's recruitment branch. It instructed me to report to the Ontario Provincial Police College on July 6, 1964. Finally, I was OPP bound. My dream of driving an OPP black-and-white would soon be realized.

But Little Barry would strike once more, and my dream of being an OPP officer nearly slipped from my grasp yet again. What a ride!

THE HOLY ANGEL TAKEDOWN

In June 1964, a month before I was to report to the OPP academy, I borrowed my dad's 1957 Ford Fairlane and went to the Royal Hotel. I drank until last call, and when I left, I decided to get a bite to eat, so I headed to the Rendezvous restaurant across from Holy Angels' Church on Talbot Street. As I pulled into a parking space, I spotted my buddies standing outside the restaurant. Little Barry, seeking attention, urged me to squeal my tires for the boys, which I did. Duh!

Although my buddies laughed hysterically at my idiotic antics, the police officers lurking in the shadows nearby were not nearly as amused. I spotted them as they crossed the street toward me. I was, to say the least, scared shit-less. *Out of the car, Ruhl!*

I tried to appear sober, but it didn't work. I was promptly arrested for impaired driving and escorted to the police station, conveniently located a block away.

My recollection of the "perp walk" is hazy. I recall telling the officers I had been accepted by the OPP but nothing else. After we arrived at the station, I stood at the counter while the officers went to an adjoining office and closed the door. They returned shortly and informed me that I could leave. Holy shit, what a relief! As I walked home, I kept thinking that I had nearly tossed a tremendous career out the window because I had let Little Barry get me so drunk that I squealed my tires just to be the centre of attention. What the hell was wrong with me?

The next morning my father poked me. He said the police called and wanted me to go to the station. With those words, my anxiety meter exploded. Oh shit, could I still be charged?

As dad and I drove to the station, I was having difficulty trying to recall the events of the previous night. I realized I had blacked out.[11]

When I entered the station, I was confronted by an angry desk sergeant who filled in the blanks. "You should be ashamed of yourself, Ruhl." He recounted the sordid details of my drunken rant at the station the night before. "If I had anything to do with it, you'd be in a cell, and your career in the OPP would be over before it began!" I realized the sergeant had probably been on duty when I acted like a drunken fool. What could I do but hang my head and apologize profusely? Thankfully, the sergeant accepted my apology.

Coincidently, I was in Port Stanley later that day and ran into one of the arresting officers. I apologized for my errant behaviour and thanked him for not charging me.

---

11   A blackout involves memory loss due to alcohol or drug abuse. It is most common with drinking too much alcohol. Blacking out from drinking is specifically associated with binge drinking. Typically, the condition is induced when a person's blood alcohol content (BAC) reaches 0.15. For comparison, it is illegal to drive with a BAC of 0.08 in nearly every state in the US. https://americanaddictioncenters.org/alcoholism-treatment/blackout

PART TWO
BOOZE WITH THE BADGE

CHAPTER 2

SUITING UP AND SHIPPING OUT

> Bad boys, bad boys watcha gonna do?
> Watcha gonna do when they come for you?
> Bad boys, bad boys watcha gonna do?
> Watcha gonna do when they come for you?
>
> – *"Bad Boys" by Ian Lewis (1987)*

THE OPP COLLEGE

I ARRIVED AT THE COLLEGE on July 6, 1964. It was located at 291 Sherbourne Street in downtown Toronto, an area known as "Cabbagetown." The area was named in the late nineteenth century when Irish immigrants grew vegetables, including cabbages, on their properties. When I entered the college, I wondered if the three-storey residence was large enough to accommodate the students.

While I waited for registration, I met Tom, who was from Windsor. He had been employed as a bartender and had competed in several amateur boxing matches in the Windsor area. Tom and I were to be roommates, bunking in the attic along with three other recruits. Once the paperwork was completed, we climbed the three flights of stairs to our room, which we discovered was somewhat sparsely furnished.

The first night in our new digs was challenging. July was hot, and the room wasn't insulated. I opened a window, which presented another problem. We were awakened by screaming sirens and traffic throughout the night. There was also the added cacophony of sporadic snoring and occasional farts. So, we didn't arise in the morning bright eyed and bushy tailed.

What better way to greet the day then eating a breakfast fit for kings, including greasy fried eggs, crispy bacon, toast, and coffee?

Following breakfast, we assembled in the classroom for orientation. We were called to attention by Superintendent (Supt.) Elmer Hoath, who entered wearing the uniform of a commissioned OPP officer. His uniform was very impressive. However, with the addition of a collage of medals emblazoned across his chest, the uniform was stunning.

He welcomed us and extended his congratulations on being selected to join the ranks of the OPP. He reviewed the course curriculum, which included motor vehicle accident investigation, investigative techniques, arrest procedures, firearms orientation, report writing, and federal and provincial legislation. Supt. Hoath added the following two advisories. "First, don't wash your underwear in the restroom sinks. Second, stay away from the bars in the vicinity of Gerrard and Sherbourne St. The 'ladies of the night' hang around that area flaunting their merchandise, and you don't want to sample it."

Our classes focused on memorizing various laws, regulations, and police procedures. Although I enjoyed my studies, I wasn't happy with the accommodations. Living with five guys can be difficult at the best of times, but to be stuffed in the stifling attic made the two weeks at the college miserable.

Shortly after arriving in Toronto, I called my mother. When she answered the phone, I could tell she was upset. She informed me that two young women who I had previously dated had been killed instantly when their vehicle spun out of control on Highway 4 near St. Thomas. I was stunned. I felt like I'd been punched in the gut.

Later that evening I went for a long walk. Apart from feeling sad, I kept thinking that my friends had died while driving an Austin Healey Sprite, like the one I owned. My mother said they were taking the vehicle for a test run. When the weekend arrived, I returned home and tried to drown my feelings barhopping, but a gut full of booze couldn't numb the sadness I felt.

When I returned to the college, our marching orders were posted on the bulletin board. I was transferred to District 16 at Port Arthur (now Thunder Bay). Since I had never been north of Parry Sound, the posting sounded like it was going to be a real adventure. I wondered if Uncle Jack was behind the transfer. I had had a dust up with him a few days prior to reporting to the college. I had been drinking with my buddies, who had a farewell party for me. Uncle Jack had just arrived and was visiting with mother. I don't recall what I said, but Jack was pissed off and exclaimed he was going to transfer me so far north that I'd need a dog sled to get around. It turned out his threat wasn't bullshit!

LONGLAC DETACHMENT

On July 31, 1964, I reported to district headquarters in Port Arthur and was given the choice of two postings to consider: communications officer at district headquarters or general duty officer at Longlac. It was a no-brainer. I wanted to be where the rubber hit the road, so I selected Longlac.

Longlac is a logging town approximately 300 kilometres northeast of Thunder Bay. The area was originally inhabited by the Ojibwa and Cree First Nations, and Kimberly-Clarke, a pulp and paper company, was the main source of employment.

When I arrived in Longlac I reserved a room at the local hotel. Then I reported for duty and met the detachment commander (det. com.) After introductions, he issued me a used uniform, a Sam Browne belt, and a holster and handcuff case. For those unfamiliar with the term, a Sam Browne belt is a wide leather belt typically found on military or police uniforms. The belt holds the gun and holster and the handcuffs in a leather case. The Sam Browne also has a one-inch wide leather strap that goes over the right shoulder to support the weight of the equipment on the belt. The corporal instructed me to put on the uniform and then return to the detachment to meet my coach officer. Anxious to get started, I hurried to the hotel and excitedly donned the uniform and equipment, then quickly removed the revolver from a weapons container. Without thinking, I loaded the gun and pulled the hammer back. As soon as I cocked the hammer, I thought, *Shit, what the hell did I just do?* I didn't know how to release the hammer! So, I carefully returned the gun to its container and walked to the detachment carrying a potentially lethal weapon.

I carefully opened the door and approached the corporal, who was sitting at his desk. "Uh, I loaded and cocked my gun," I said, "and I don't know how to release the hammer." I'll never forget the bewildered look on his face. I can only imagine what he was thinking: *Who the hell did they send me, Barney Fife?*[12]

Without comment, the corporal carefully removed the weapon from the container and released the hammer. "I assume you didn't have guns when you were growing up?" he said.

---

12   The incompetent cop on the Andy Griffith 1960s TV sitcom.

"No, I never had any interest in them," I replied. He nodded and then proceeded to review the firearm safety instructions. I must say he had a very attentive student.

The following day, I met the detachment members who took me under their collective wing. In addition to familiarizing me with the detachment area, they showed me the haunts of the active criminals.

For the first couple of weeks, I roomed at the Trans-Canada Hotel. Then I moved into the Kimberley-Clarke bunkhouse. I also stopped eating at a local restaurant after hearing about Ma White's Boarding House. She was an excellent chef and charged a paltry 75 cents for her delicious fare. To show my appreciation, I paid her a dollar, and other diners followed suit.

Sunday was always a special day at Ma White's. Her delicious offerings included turkey, mounds of mashed potatoes, succulent cabbage rolls, and blueberry or cherry pie with homemade ice cream. Yum, my mouth is watering as I write. The diners at Ma Whites were Kimberley-Clarke employees and a few OPP officers. The Kimberley-Clarke employees, who worked in the bush, appeared to be in excellent physical condition. I frequently wondered how the hell I'd arrest them if they resisted. Thankfully, I never had to learn the answer to that question.

Winters in Longlac were bone-chillingly cold. When I finished an evening shift, I was required to leave the cruiser attached to a block-heater at the detachment and walk to the bunkhouse. Sometimes the temperature was -42°C. Nevertheless, I enjoyed the solitude, the snow, which sparkled like diamonds, the smoke rising from the chimneys, and the sound of wolves howling in the distance. When I arrived at the bunkhouse, I'd hoist a few and drink some vodka, neat. Nobody from the detachment knew I was a souse!

However, one person became aware of my excessive drinking. Walter was the custodian at the bunkhouse. He was in his mid-fifties and had emigrated from Poland in the late 1950s. When Walter and I met, he invited me to his room to show off his impressive coin collection and offered me a shot of Crown Royal, which I didn't turn down. As I savored the drink, I looked around and noticed he had few family photographs. After a few more shots, Walter related that his wife had refused to join him in Canada. He began crying, which caused me to feel uncomfortable, so much so that I left him crying alone.[13]

---

13   The reason I feel badly now about leaving Walter alone when he was crying is because, some twenty years later, I trained and served as an OPP peer supporter and then as an addiction counsellor. The role of a police peer supporter is to support and assist police officers and civilians who are experiencing emotional difficulties. In Walter's case, however, I had had no such training, and all I could think to do at the time was to leave him alone.

However, Walter and I became boozing buddies and polished off many bottles of Crown Royal together. Unfortunately, whenever he got hammered, he recalled fond memories of his life in Poland and began crying! That was my cue to leave him alone. He was a very lonely man who missed his wife, and no amount of booze could heal that emotional wound.

When I left Longlac, Walter gave me a 1965 Canadian dollar as a parting gift. I have often wondered what became of my boozing buddy.

Drinking in Longlac was OK, but it was not the amount that Little Barry desired. I was always fearful that the detachment personnel would discover my "secret." So, every six weeks I travelled to Port Arthur, where I drank like the proverbial "drunken sailor." I usually stayed at a downtown hotel and frequented the many watering holes in the area. In the evenings, I liked to attend Club 17, where sometimes I got lucky! When the weekend was over, I'd board a bus for Longlac, nursing a hangover and feeling depressed. Another lost weekend.

MY FIRST MAJOR INVESTIGATION

On a particularly frigid January evening, my partner and I were observing patrons leaving the Longlac Hotel. The corporal had instructed us to park in the CNR lot, so patrons exiting the hotel would see us and behave. The hotel is located on the north side of the CNR railway tracks, which was particularly troubling because patrons leaving the hotel had to cross the tracks to reach Highway 11. We were shooting the breeze when an eastbound four-engine freight train roared past the Longlac station.

"I hope nobody gets in front of that rocket!" I joked. The words were no sooner out of my mouth when the station master ran toward us, yelling. "Someone's been hit!"

The train came to a screeching stop a quarter mile east of the hotel. When we arrived on the scene, we were greeted by a horrific sight. I found various body parts scattered along the tracks, including a ghastly severed hand. The corporal directed me to investigate. Suddenly, a sense of dread washed over me. This was my first major investigation and trial by fire. Was I up to the task?

I learned that Mr. Ladimer Kozinski* and his buddies from work had been drinking for most of the evening. (A subsequent autopsy revealed his blood alcohol concentration (BAC) was 0.37 mg of alcohol per 100 ml of blood. As a matter of interest, blood alcohol levels between 0.35 and 0.40 typically result in a level of impairment achieved by surgical anesthesia. People who consume that quantity often pass out or stop breathing.[14])

When we completed the investigation, the team went to the twenty-four-hour diner in town. Without thinking, I ordered a large bowl of stew. When the steaming meal arrived, I was introduced to the "gallows humour" cops, resort to as a means of relieving stress when the other officers started comparing the stew to Mr. Kozinski's body parts. I didn't let them know that their macabre banter bothered me, and amidst their laughter, I ate in silence.

When I returned to my room, I was flooded with the horrific images I had seen on the tracks. I'd never seen a mutilated body before, and I couldn't get the gruesome images out of my head no matter how much I drank. I had never heard of post-traumatic stress (PTS), so I didn't understand that what I was experiencing was a normal reaction to a very traumatic event.

When a person encounters a life event that is far outside the norms of what they have experienced, the incident evokes strong visceral and emotional reactions as their brain attempts to make sense of the experience. One of the ways the brain attempts to cope is by reliving or re-experiencing the event. That is a natural human reaction to a traumatic event as the person tries to make sense of the tragedy based on pre-existing information. In most instances, the traumatic reactions diminish after a few days. However, troublesome reactions might persist for more than thirty days, and the person would likely benefit from professional assistance. Police officers and other first responders frequently encounter traumatic events not easily assimilated into prior experiences, and they struggle to rid themselves of the disturbing reactions associated with them. Unfortunately, I chose drinking to cope with my traumatic reactions. I learned later that drinking is a common way for many officers to cope with their traumatic symptoms.[15] Unfortunately, alcohol is not an effective coping method and can lead to substance abuse issues.

I was tasked with locating Mr. Kozinski's next of kin. Sadly, he didn't have any relatives. Essentially, I couldn't find one person to celebrate his life or mourn his death. Because, he didn't have any relatives, his estate became the property of the Ontario Public Trustee. (When I was looking for assets, I discovered hundreds of uncashed cheques issued to him by Kimberly-Clarke. By default, this money also became the property of the Ontario Public Trustee.)

---

14   https://www.alcohol.org/effects/blood-alcohol-concentration/

15   OPP peer support training provided by Dr. David Hoath, OPP Psychologist.

Mr. Kozinski's tragic demise lingered with me for a long time. In fact, to this day, fifty-one years later, I can still picture those ghastly images. Thankfully, I no longer experience the emotional turmoil when recalling his horrific death.

AN UNWELCOME TRANSFER

In May 1965, I received notification that I had been transferred to Meaford in District 6, effective June 1.

"It looks like Uncle Jack wants you closer to home," the corporal joked as he handed me the notification. I didn't find his wisecrack amusing. I enjoyed working at Longlac and was involved in some interesting criminal investigations. I have no doubt that my uncle facilitated the transfer. I guess he had been monitoring my progress and thought it would be "safe" to transfer me to a southern detachment. I wish he had contacted me first though. It simply wasn't right! Other officers had requested transfers and been turned down. They had paid their dues and were justified in feeling they were deserving. Meanwhile, I had received the coveted transfer because my uncle was the assistant commissioner. The "elephant" in the office caused the palpable tension to linger like an ominous cloud. I missed the jocular camaraderie that I had shared with the detachment personnel, and I thought everyone was talking behind my back. I felt shitty and couldn't wait to leave.

The evening before my departure, the corporal invited the officers to his residence for drinks, but it seemed everyone, including the chatty corporal, was uneasy. I had been at other soirees replete with laughter and camaraderie, but this was different. It seemed that all the oxygen had been sucked out of the room. It felt like I was at a wake! A few officers attempted to break the ice by recounting hilarious cop stories, but their efforts fell on deaf ears. Thankfully, after a couple of agonizing hours, everyone was ready to leave. We said our goodbyes, and as I walked to the bunkhouse for the last time, I was emotionally spent.

The next morning, I settled in for the twenty-hour trek to Toronto. I gazed out the window as the train gathered speed and watched with mixed emotions as Longlac disappeared into the distance. When it was out of sight, my thoughts turned to the future. I wondered what kind of reception I'd receive at Meaford.

WELCOME TO MEAFORD

Meaford is a picturesque town on the southern shores of Georgian Bay, east of Owen Sound. It's a hot spot for fishing, and nearby are three popular ski resorts. The Meaford Tank Range (now known as the Land Force Central Area Training Centre) is five kilometres, northwest of town. A popular attraction in the centre of town is "Beautiful Joe" Park. It was named in memory of a much-loved dog named Joe who was featured in the book *Beautiful Joe*, authored by Margaret Marshall Saunders.

A priority when I arrived in Meaford was finding a place to stay. I happened to mention my dilemma to a guy named Ralph, who worked at a local bank. He suggested talking to his landlady, who was looking for another boarder. Later that day, I dropped by her residence and was greeted by an elderly woman with an engaging smile. She showed me around, and it was obvious the place needed a facelift. The house had a small kitchen, living room, and bathroom on the main floor and two small bedrooms upstairs.

When we finished the tour, we had a cup of tea. When she learned I was an OPP officer, she smiled. I knew I was in! However, she wanted to know if I smoked or drank. I told her I had the occasional cigarette and glass of wine, which seemed to satisfy her. She offered me the room for $45 per week. So, thanks to Ralph, I had a place to live. Nevertheless, I knew the arrangement was short term.

BEDDING DOWN AND BOOZING UP

Ralph and I became buddies. I discovered he liked cribbage, my favorite card game. He also liked drinking. So, we spent many a night playing cribbage and drinking without disturbing our teetotaler landlady. To make the game more interesting, we played for five cents a point, and between shots of rye and ribbing each other, we had a blast. Unfortunately, Ralph couldn't keep up with me. So, when he needed to "ralph," a garbage can was nearby. We ultimately discovered that our wins and losses balanced out. However, even when I lost, I had the last laugh because I always made the cheques payable to Ralph "the Loser" Jackson* drawn on his bank!

I knew it was time to move on when our busybody landlady insisted on quizzing me about my investigations. Ralph tagged along with me. We found a spacious apartment overlooking scenic Georgian Bay. It wasn't a problem finding furniture because Ralph knew an auctioneer who liked a drink. So, with booze in hand, we paid him a visit and managed to outfit our new digs for $50.

HOUSE "WARNING" PARTY

After moving in, we invited friends over for drinks. I invited officers from the detachment and a few town cops, including the chief. We had a well-stocked bar, and with the booze flowing, the party was rolling.

As the evening progressed, everyone seemed to be having a boozy good time. Nevertheless, I thought we needed music, so I selected the "William Tell Overture" to play on a record player that I had just bought. In my wasted state, I thought it would be a "neighborly gesture" to crank up the volume, so the neighborhood could listen to William Tell! Surprisingly, no one liked the gesture at 2:00 a.m. Who knew?

Our reverie was interrupted by a very annoyed police sergeant who had received several noise complaints. He had also heard the blaring music two blocks away! After I offered a profound apology, I noticed him spot his chief amongst the drunken revelers. With a tip of his hat, he retreated from the apartment with no further comment. Not long after, our guests departed, bringing our soiree to an abrupt end. Obviously, I had screwed up big time. I managed to get totally wasted, ruin the party, and piss off the neighborhood and the police sergeant. And to think I had just arrived in town!

MEAFORD DETACHMENT

Meaford had the same complement of officers as Longlac. The detachment commander held the rank of corporal and supervised six constables. When I was introduced to the other members, I wondered if they were aware of my "fixed" transfer. Regardless of what they knew, I was determined to show my stuff and hit the road running!

I checked the gravel pits, apple orchards, and back roads and usually returned to the detachment with liquor seizures. My first seizure involved soldiers from the Meaford Tank Range. I was patrolling on Concession 4, south of Meaford, behind a slow-moving vehicle. I pulled it over and discovered the three occupants were soldiers from the tank range. When the driver rolled down his window, I detected the smell of alcohol, and the occupants looked like they had been caught with their hands in the cookie jar. Based on my "cruising days," I was sure there was booze in the car. So, I used a pitch I had perfected in Longlac.

"OK, boys, I'm sure there's booze in the car, so this is what we're going to do. If you hand it over, I'll charge one of you with possession, and you can split the fine. However, if I need to search the vehicle, I'll charge each of you with possession." As expected, the soldiers handed over the beer without comment. I served the soldier who fessed up with a ticket.

A few months later, I had a bizarre encounter with another soldier from the range. In this instance, I was dispatched to Concession 7, St. Vincent Township, to investigate the report of a military jeep in a ditch. When I arrived on the scene, I noted that there were two jeeps in the ditch, which seemed odd because only one soldier was present. Somewhat sheepishly, the soldier explained that he had taken the first jeep for a ride and ditched it. Thinking, he could handle the situation on his own, he hitchhiked to the range and stole a second jeep. His plan was to use the second jeep to pull the first jeep out of the ditch. With no one to help, he managed to ditch the second jeep too. Consequently, he was charged with two counts of taking a vehicle without the owner's consent under the Criminal Code.

THE BARRISTER'S SHITTY SHOES

I appeared in magistrates court frequently and became acquainted with several trial lawyers, including Ross*, a barrister from Owen Sound. Ross enjoyed drinking as much as me, and occasionally, we dropped into the Legion hall for a drink after court.

One day, Ross asked me for a lift to Owen Sound. I wasn't scheduled to work until 5:00, so I agreed. Big mistake!

Prior to leaving Meaford, we stopped at the liquor store, where Ross bought a mickey of lemon gin. We polished it off before reaching the Owen Sound city limits. Now that Ross had wet his whistle, he wanted to treat me to lunch at a mom-and-pop diner on the west side of town. When we entered the diner, a friendly waitress greeted Ross with a big smile and a hug. We ordered lunch and, much to my surprise, Ross ordered a couple of beers.

"Ross," I exclaimed, "this place doesn't have a bar."

He smiled. "I know, but there's always booze stashed in the kitchen for me." He added that he held a mortgage on the place. The waitress brought our orders and two bottles of beer. I was uptight because some customers noticed the beer. I managed to wolf down my meal, but I just wanted to get the hell out of there!

Ross paid the bill and then ordered two beers to go. When we were walking to the car, I noticed he was pissed! I wanted to take him home, but he wanted no part of that! Instead, he asked me to take him to Chatsworth, about 15 km south of Owen Sound, to check on some calves that he had purchased recently. I was getting peeved because I was scheduled to work at 5:00, and I was feeling resentful that he was taking advantage me.

When we arrived at the compound, I noticed the ground was covered with bovine excretions, otherwise known as cow shit. Despite my warning for "the urban cowboy" to stay out of the compound, he didn't listen. I watched in horror as he stumbled through the cow shit, patting the yearlings on their rumps. He almost fell into the shitty mud bath! When he got back into my pristine and recently purchased Mustang, his shoes were caked with dung, and he reeked of shit. To add insult to injury, he hawked a gob of chewing tobacco at the *closed* passenger window. Fuck! I watched the disgusting blotch of spittle seep into the sill, leaving a trail of slime in its wake. Enraged, I quickly drove the stinking "cowboy" to his residence. I returned to Meaford and managed to catch a couple of hours of sleep before enforcing the law, including the ones I had just broken.

SELF-REFLECTION

As I write this, I can't help but wonder why I didn't speak up to Ross. Perhaps I was fearful of not being liked and accepted, which stems from low self-esteem. At that time, I needed to be liked and accepted by everyone, coworkers and lawyers included. I was willing to ingratiate myself with this drunken lawyer, who didn't give a rat's ass for me or my car. Even though I was maturing as a police officer, I didn't feel secure enough to speak up for myself, and I was mad at myself for not doing it. Nevertheless, my fear of not being accepted continued to control my life and my drinking for some time to come.

OUT OF THE MOUTH OF BABES

I investigated many motor vehicle collisions while stationed in Meaford, most of which were relatively minor. However, we did have the occasional fatal collision, A young man was returning from work when his car careened off the road and struck a tree. He was killed instantly. The reason I recall this collision so vividly is because I was assigned to notify the next of kin of his death.

I was very uptight. Although I received plenty of information during recruit training, death notifications were not on the syllabus. During the nail-biting trip to his house, my mind was racing. *What should I say? What should I do? What if I say something wrong, something stupid? What if...?* Suddenly, I spotted a mailbox displaying the deceased man's name. It was showtime.

I drove slowly down the lane, and my heart began pounding when I spotted the residence. As I approached, a woman and a young boy were standing inside the screen door. I exited the cruiser, and by then the adrenalin had kicked in, and my heart was beating like a jackhammer.

"Oh, I heard the car and thought it was my husband returning from work," the woman said.

Jesus, this isn't going to be easy, I thought.

She came out of the house and stood on the porch holding the boy's hand. In a death notification, the first thing to do is ensure that the person is related to the deceased, so I started by confirming that William Small* was her husband. When she responded that he was, I continued. "I'm so sorry to have to inform you that William was killed in a car accident west of here about an hour ago." She appeared stunned by the tragic news. She remained silent for several seconds. Then her eyes filled with tears, and she began to sob uncontrollably. I stood there feeling helpless. *What the hell do I do? What do I say?*

Suddenly, I heard the small boy's trembling, timid voice. "Don't cry, Mommy. I'll get you a new daddy." I almost lost it. The devastated woman put her arm around her son, and they walked slowly into the house. I stayed with her until a relative arrived from Collingwood. I sat there hoping he had a heavy foot because I was stressed watching the grief-stricken widow vacillate between sobbing and breaking into mournful cries, all the while cradling her son.

Finally, her brother-in-law arrived, and I gave him my information should the family have any questions. As I returned to the detachment, I couldn't stop thinking about the little boy's promise to his mother to get her a new "daddy." Even now when I recall that mournful moment, I get a lump in my throat.

When I returned to my apartment, I opened a bottle of rye. I don't know if you've ever heard the expression "the bottle is my best friend," but that evening, the bottle and I hunkered down together. The best thing about a bottle of booze is that it's nonjudgmental. So, I used my "booze buddy" to placate the unsettling memories of my first death notification.

As my career progressed, I made several more death notifications. It was always difficult: the knock on the door, the notification, and witnessing the anguish when a family member heard their loved one had died. Fast-forward to 1994. During my exit interview, I recommended that the OPP college include compassionate notifications in their training syllabus. It's inconceivable that something as important as death notifications were never included in the curriculum.

SELF-REFLECTION

Back in my nascent alcoholic days, drinking until I was drunk seemed like the right thing to do. Heck, maybe I thought it was the only thing to do. Essentially, drown or dampen the emotional chaos I was feeling after having to inform someone that their loved one was dead. I didn't realize that almost all police officers struggle emotionally with this task, but I never shared the emotional pain I was feeling. I didn't think that anyone would care or understand. Either that or they might ridicule me for being soft or a wussy. And to a certain degree, I was probably right. Sharing concerns wasn't acceptable amongst members. In fact, if I had shared my thoughts and feelings about the difficulty I was experiencing, I might have been laughed at or ridiculed. However, today peer-support officers are trained to listen to and support officers who are emotionally affected after such calls. I became a peer supporter. So, if you are reading this book and wondering how to cope with your first death notification, contact a peer supporter, and share your thoughts. And when you complete that first death notification, don't get drunk. Trust me, it doesn't help!

BOOZY BATTLES

The OPP were given a substantial pay raise in 1966. Coincidently, on the day it was announced, a retirement party was being held for the chief of the Collingwood Police Service. Party! My supervisor, whom I shall refer to as Corporal E., and my partner and I decided to attend and bid the chief farewell.

The party was at the Mountain View Hotel, a Collingwood watering hole. It was well underway when we arrived, and since I had already drank a couple of "wobbly pops," it wasn't long before I was feeling no pain and talking up a storm—which led to another storm!

I'm not sure what I said, but apparently, I pissed off a hulk of a cop from Collingwood, who was approximately 6 feet 6 inches and 250 pounds. Ironically, he was known as the "Gentle Giant," but not that night. Whatever I said brought out his inner "Hulk." He lifted me off the floor and, as I dangled like a marionette, slammed his massive fist into my ribs, causing me to double over, then slammed me to the floor. I was rescued by my cohorts, who poured me into the cruiser. I was dazed and hurting, so I didn't need to hear Corporal E. bad-mouthing Uncle Jack. His venomous attack was relentless and peppered with profanity. Then he started on me. Without much thought, I told him to keep his goddamn mouth shut.

"If you're such a tough guy, Ruhl, let's get it on!" he said. Pissed off, I told my partner to pull over. Unfortunately, he did.

Corporal E. was the first one out of the cruiser. As I stepped out, he coldcocked me. I fell to my knees, dazed, and extremely enraged, I leapt off the ground and launched a haymaker. Luckily, the blow found its target, causing Corporal E. to stumble backwards into the dense brush. Then he took off running.

Holy shit! I thought. *I just punched out my supervisor!* We frantically searched the area but couldn't find him. (We found out later that he had called an off-duty officer to pick him up.)

The next morning, I awoke hungover and contrite. *What the hell is wrong with me?* I wondered. *I got shit-faced, made an ass of myself at the chief's party, and punched out my boss.* I was in panic mode attempting to decide what I should do. I ran through my options: call in sick and knock back some vodka or go to work and face the music. Although I was hungover, I decided the only option was to go to work.

I didn't eat breakfast because that would have created a barf rebellion. I walked slowly to the detachment, ruminating about my fucked-up shitshow. Even though my head was pounding, I still had enough functioning brain cells left to wonder what Corporal E. was going to do, and I didn't think a hug was an option. I knew I was in for a rough ride.

When I was within eyesight of the detachment, my heart began to pound, and I was sweating profusely. I reluctantly entered the office and came face to face with Corporal E. He was shuffling papers at his desk and was sporting a Band-Aid on his forehead. When our eyes met, I didn't know what the hell to say or do. Suddenly, he got up from his desk and walked toward me with his hand extended. I was so dumbfounded that I don't recall what was said. Nevertheless, the handshake said it all, and he suggested I take the day off, which sounded like a good idea.

The next day, I was approached by an officer from the detachment who hadn't been at the party. He said he had heard about what happened and was going to report the incident to Mount Forest District Headquarters. I told him to keep his mouth shut, and he did. I didn't think Corporal E. wanted the brass to learn he had been bad-mouthing Assistant Commissioner Jack Whitty!

One would think after getting stupid drunk and punching out my supervisor, I would have heeded the wake-up call. Nope! Just a couple of months later, I was transporting a prisoner to court in Owen Sound with my partner. Imagine this scenario: my partner and our prisoner witnessing me puking my guts out on the shoulder of Highway 26. But I'm getting ahead of myself.

The unpleasantry was the result of a celebration following the arrest of a career criminal for armed robbery. He was wanted for a violent home invasion in Euphrasia Township south of Meaford. The bad guy had a lengthy criminal record and was known to carry weapons. I had been looking for him and received reliable information from an informant that he was holed up at a vacant farmhouse in the Markdale area. My partner and I headed there hoping to nab him before nightfall. The informant thought he was at a vacant farm on Concession 7, just outside of Markdale, but he was unsure of the exact location. Our search was futile, until my partner spotted smoke billowing from a house behind a dense thicket of brush. Was this his hideaway?

We ditched the cruiser and crept toward the dilapidated house. As we neared the building, the terrifying thought of being involved in a shoot-out flooded my psyche. We stepped carefully onto the porch, causing the floorboards to creak. *Shit, did he hear us?* I wondered. *Is he even here? Does he have a gun pointed at the door?* For a split second, I considered backing off and waiting for backup, but I knew they would arrive after dark, making the bust even more dangerous. No, it was showtime!

I nodded at my partner, and with my heart pounding, gingerly tried the doorknob. *Holy shit! It's unlocked!* I quietly opened the door, and we entered with weapons drawn. We crept along the darkened hallway. Then I heard a sound that seemed to be coming from a room with the door partially ajar. We quietly approached and flung it open. Bingo! A very stunned bad guy was sitting on the toilet! Yes, we literally caught him with his pants down on the potty! I think we scared the shit out of him. He didn't resist even though he had a hunting knife on his belt, So, after returning to Meaford and locking him up, it was time to celebrate by hoisting a few! I invited some officers from the detachment over for a few drinks, which turned out to be many more than a few.

I awoke the next morning with a pounding headache and a queasy stomach. Not the ideal condition for attending court! My partner picked me up, and with the prisoner on board, we headed for Owen Sound. It wasn't long before I knew I was going to puke. My mouth began to water, and I tried to distract myself by looking at the trees along the highway. That didn't work.

"Stop the car," I exclaimed. My partner pulled onto the shoulder, and I jumped out and retched. Feeling somewhat better, I returned to the cruiser, and we resumed our journey. I always wondered what my traveling companions thought. That was not my finest hour!

SELF-REFLECTION

Clearly, you can see that I am an alcoholic, a rip-roaring drunk. Nevertheless, the possibility that I was an alcoholic never crossed my mind. Why? Because, I was still in control, or so I thought. Everyone drinks, don't they? Everybody pukes from drinking every now and again, don't they? I was young, robust, and on the move, and I was making a name for myself as a good cop.

MOVING ON

I began to wonder if my reputation was becoming the topic of the town and thought maybe I should consider getting out of Dodge. I got the answer in the form of an exciting memorandum. In 1967, Canada was hosting Expo 67 in Montreal, and the OPP was looking for officers to serve at the Ontario Pavilion. Now, *that's for me*, I thought and quickly applied. The candidates had to be single and speak French. I was single, but "Je ne parle pas francais." I decided to throw my hat in the ring anyway.

Shortly after submitting my application, I received word that I was to be interviewed by the superintendent and sergeant major at district headquarters in Mount Forest. Although I was excited to get an interview, I was also anxious. What if they asked me to speak French? The interview was brief, and it seemed like the brass were only interested in how I looked wearing the blue. They gave me the once-over, and I boldly suggested that if I were selected, I should be issued a new uniform! Amazingly, they accepted my assurance that I spoke French without further question or comment. (My French was limited to a few words, such as "oui," "non," "s'il vous plais," "a la gauche," and "a la droit.") I thanked the command staff for the interview, and then I waited.

On April 13, I received notification from E. W. Miller, Chief Superintendent of Field Operations, that I had been accepted for the Expo 67 detail. I was instructed to report to Sergeant J. C. Hawkins at the Laurentian Hotel in downtown Montreal on April 19. Twenty-eight officers had been selected, and I was proud to be one of them. Montreal was to become home until the exposition closed on October 27, 1967.

CHAPTER 3
EXPO 67

> Give us a place to stand
> And a place to grow
> And call this land Ontario…
> Ontari-ari-ari-o!
>
> – *"A Place to Stand" by Dolores Claman*

THE DAY I ARRIVED AT the Expo site it was exciting to step onto the stage where the world was on display. I was proud to have been selected to represent Ontario. I rode the monorail to our pavilion and marveled at the other pavilions, representing sixty-two countries. When the curtain came down on this magnificent exposition, approximately 50 million people had visited.

BOOZING BUDDIES

The Ontario government arranged accommodation for officers at "Habitat 67" and two residences in Ville Brossard on the South Shore. Habitat 67 was an innovative complex consisting of 158 interlocking apartments and was designed by Montreal architect Moshe Safdie. I was one of five officers assigned to a semi-detached residence in Ville Brossard.

On my first shopping excursion with the other officers, we filled three shopping carts with groceries and beer. When we returned to our new digs, we popped a beer and became acquainted. I learned that my roommate, Rick*, also enjoyed drinking. So, sometimes after work we barhopped on the south shore, hoping to get lucky!

On an evening I would like to forget, we invited a couple of women we met at a bar to our place. Upon reflection, it was a dumb idea. Four drunken revelers pouring into the residence when our roommates were asleep! Undeterred, we lit the party stick and carried on. But our drunken exuberance woke our slumbering roommates, who proceeded to chew us out. There was no "happy ending" when we drove the women home.

The next morning, I was greeted with hostile stares from my roomies. As we drove to the pavilion, their silence was deafening. Predictably, I was hungover throughout the shift and was not the finest host when inquisitive tourists asked me questions about the pavilion.

"Wouldn't a cold one taste good?" Rick whispered at one point. The thought of quaffing a beer was stuck in my psyche for the remainder of the shift.

DINNER WITH UNCLE JACK

Assistant Commissioner Jack Whitty visited the Expo detachment in August. After he inspected the officers, he invited me to dinner. Even though he was my uncle, I felt honored to be invited out to dinner by the assistant commissioner of the OPP.

When I arrived at the hotel where he was staying, he was already in the bag. He was able to discuss the Expo detail until we drained a bottle of rye, but a pending disaster was about to unfold.

"Let's get some Chinese food," he said. Although I was also in the bag, it was obvious he was in no shape to leave the hotel, so I suggested take-out. "No, let's go out," he said, slurring his words. "There's a Chinese restaurant around the corner."

When we left the hotel, we met some OPP officers on St. Catherine Street. During the brief conversation, Jack struggled to be coherent. I was embarrassed for him and me.

After the officers left, we arrived at the restaurant, and the maître d' escorted us to a booth. I noticed this wasn't a typical Chinese restaurant. It was a cut above and adorned with ornate oriental artifacts.

After the waiter took our order, Jack staggered to the restroom and barely managed to stay upright on his return. And as we waited for the food, I was beginning to feel very anxious, because I never knew what he might say or do. Sure enough. when our waiter passed the table, Jack shouted, "Hey, boy, where's our food?" Although not surprised, I was embarrassed and enraged. When I tuned into the chatter from diners around us, it was obvious they weren't impressed by Jack's racist remark. Unfortunately, the waiter heard him and appeared startled. Still, Jack either didn't realize or didn't care that he had uttered such a derogatory remark.

Finally, dinner arrived. Normally, I would have enjoyed the succulent offerings, but considering what had occurred, I had lost my appetite. The occasional glances from the other diners added to my discomfort. I was hoping Jack would eat quickly, so we could leave. Regrettably, he was taking his time. In his drunken condition, he was having problems transporting the food from the plate to his mouth. Finally, he finished, leaving the plate half eaten. Relieved, I paid the bill, leaving a substantial tip. I was thankful the hotel was nearby because Jack was having difficulty staying upright. When we arrived at the hotel, I put him on the bed, and he quickly passed out.

The following morning, he called and thanked me for dining with him. He didn't mention the restaurant or his racist comment. Nevertheless, I considered his behaviour unacceptable.

SELF-REFLECTION

Now, that I'm writing this, I can see similarities in Uncle Jack's behaviour and some of my own. I reflect on the time when I was so drunk that I dyed my hair orange or cursed the officers who arrested me for impaired driving prior to entering the OPP. You might think my uncle's antics would have motivated me to reconsider my aberrant behaviour, but that didn't happen. Why? That is the insidious nature of denial in the life of an alcoholic. Jack saw himself as having a good time. He was incapable of standing outside of his drunkenness and judging his behaviour. Similarly, I never saw my previous actions or the behaviour I was likely to display in the future as those of an alcoholic. Alcoholics are addicted to alcohol, but they also suffer from a type of psychological blindness that protects and prolongs their drinking. However, if someone admits that he or she is an alcoholic, really admits it, the person must commit to radical change or, by default, admit and accept that he or she is self-destructive.

VISITING UNCLE HUEY

During our visit, Uncle Jack asked me to visit Huey McGovern, his late Aunt Annie's husband. Annie had died recently, and Huey lived alone in Lachine on the south shore of Montreal Island. Jack thought Huey would enjoy some company, and I was eager to meet him because I recalled with fondness how he and Annie sent my brothers and me a gift of money every Christmas.

Shortly after Jack returned to Ontario, I arranged to visit Huey on the weekend. Huey was in his eighties and lived in an older section of Lachine, Quebec. When I knocked, I was somewhat surprised to be greeted by a tall, robust man with a firm handshake. Huey greeted me with a cheerful smile, and I was relieved to find that it was easy to talk to him. He was very inquisitive and wanted to know about my life's journey. Furthermore, he seemed genuinely delighted when I thanked him for the money that he and Annie had sent us at Christmas. He related that since they were childless, they enjoyed sending us the annual gifts.

After a few drinks, Huey asked me to take him shopping. I drove him to a plaza near his residence, and he purchased some groceries and a forty-pounder of rye. We returned to his home and swapped stories over many drinks. In the process, I learned a great deal about my mother's parents. I was particularly curious about my Grandfather Leo because I vaguely recalled Uncle Jack mentioning he wasn't able to maintain employment. I wondered if he abused alcohol.

Puffing on a stinky cigarillo, Huey related that Leo was a heavy drinker, which worried my Grandmother Florence. Leo had been a conductor with the Canadian National Railway (CNR), but apparently, his drinking had become problematic, and despite numerous unheeded warnings, he was eventually fired. Since Leo was the sole breadwinner, Florence implored Huey to intervene. Huey was well known in Ontario and was able to get Leo employment with the Canadian Pacific Railway (CPR) constructing the iconic Royal York Hotel in Toronto. Unfortunately, Leo was caught drinking on the job and was fired. For Huey, that was the last straw, and he severed ties. Leo died in 1961 at the age of seventy-two. By then he was homeless, and my parents invited him to stay at our home before he died.

The evening was enlightening and intoxicating. We managed to polish off the forty-pounder, so I wisely stayed overnight. When I awoke the next morning, I smelled bacon and found Huey preparing breakfast. The meal was delicious even though I was nursing a hangover. Between bites, Huey fondly recalled preparing breakfast for Annie. After we finished, he showed me some photographs of them. They appeared to have had a wonderful relationship. Even though I was enjoying the visit, I needed to return to Ville Brossard. Huey pleaded with me to stay a little longer. I could tell he was very lonely and missing Annie, so I promised to visit him in a couple of weeks.

I visited Huey during the summer and a couple of days before leaving Expo. We had a great visit, and before I left, he handed me an envelope containing a $20 bill along with a note that read, "Thanks Barry, Uncle Huey." I didn't understand why he gave me the money. However, after thinking about it, I realized it was because he and Annie had gifted my brothers and me every Christmas, and it may have helped him feel emotionally closer to Annie's memory. Huey died in 1969 at the age of eighty-nine. "Carpe Diem" could have been his credo.

SELF-REFLECTION

Until my visit with Huey, I didn't know much about my mother's side of the family. I knew that Uncle Jack, my mother's brother, was an alcoholic. However, I had no idea my maternal grandfather was also an alcoholic. This should have been a cause for concern because my father was also an alcoholic, but I continued to drink, jeopardizing my health, my career, and my marriage.

HOISTING THE STANLEY CUP

Officers were assigned to one of the many attractions throughout the pavilion, including the theatre, the art gallery, and the Stanley Cup exhibit. To minimize the boredom, we changed positions every few hours. The two most popular attractions were the 540-seat circular theatre and the Stanley Cup exhibit. The theatre featured a multi-image 16-mm film entitled *A Place to Stand* that highlighted Ontario's social and economic development. The Stanley Cup exhibit was my personal favourite. The year was 1967, and the Toronto Maple Leafs had defeated their arch-rivals, the Montreal Canadiens. Much to the chagrin of our Quebec neighbours, the Stanley Cup was on display at our pavilion for the duration of Expo. So, when Quebecers visited the pavilion, they would stare at the exhibit and ask, "La Coupe Stanley?"

"Oui, La Coupe Stanley," I replied. Although undocumented, I probably handled the cup more than any player in the NHL. That is, the cup was stored in the detachment office after hours for safekeeping. If I was working when the pavilion closed, I was frequently assigned to take the Cup to the detachment office. Unfortunately, I was never photographed holding it.

The author at the Ontario Pavilion, Expo 67
(Credit: Barry Ruhl)

It didn't take long for the novelty of standing at a post to become mind-numbing monotony. This was particularly true whenever I was hungover. The booze cycle at our residence was relentless. I would party with anyone who showed up and then grab a few hours of shuteye before reporting for duty with the predictable hangover. And the "bar" never closed, especially when friends from Ontario popped in. I'd return home after working a midnight shift and be greeted by a horde of visitors quaffing beer on our front lawn. Of course, I joined them. With only a few hours of shuteye, I'd be back in the "bag[16]" for the next midnight shift.

MEMORIES OF PREMIER JOHN ROBARTS

One of our functions was security for VIPs. The Ontario government was hosting a cocktail party for dignitaries from around the world. Not surprisingly, Premier John Robarts was present and brought along his young son, Timothy. I watched the premier stroll around the grounds with his arm around his son. Clearly, they were close, and Robarts really loved his son. But whenever I remember the premier and his son, I can't help but recall what happened in the coming years.

---

16   A term commonly used by police officers to refer to their uniform.

Sadly, in 1972, Timothy committed suicide near Woodstock at the age of twenty-one.[17] He left a twelve-page, single-spaced letter and blamed no one for his actions. He wrote that "he felt that he wasn't cut out for the world." Tragically, ten years later, on October 18, 1982, John Robarts walked into the shower at his residence in Toronto and took his own life with a shotgun that the Ontario Progressive Conservative party had presented to him for his years of public service. Unfortunately, I cannot think of Expo 67 without recalling the tragic passing of John and Timothy Robarts. To this day, I am befuddled by the act of suicide and the tremendous burden of loss, guilt, and anger that remains with those who are left behind.

THE FAREWELL PARTY

The months passed quickly, and before I knew it, the curtain was about to fall on Expo 67. To celebrate the closing, the OPP contingent staged a farewell party at Habitat 67. Emblematic of their respective pavilions, many other hosts and hostesses arrived wearing their uniforms. As the party gathered momentum, everyone was noshing on appetizers and sipping cocktails. Nevertheless, something was missing: music. I knew Claude Boulet, deputy director of operations at the pavilion, had a stereo in his unit, so Rick and I knocked on his door, but no one answered. The door was unlocked, so we thought it would be OK if we "borrowed" it. When we entered party central muscling the large music box, we were greeted with applause and laughter by the revelers.

The music was blaring, and I was dancing up a storm when suddenly, out of the corner of my eye, I caught a glimpse of Claude staring at his stereo. *Oh shit,* I thought, *how will I fix this?* I approached Claude in a contrite manner. "Hi, Claude. I hope you don't mind, but we didn't have music, and what's a party without it, eh?"

Fortunately for Rick and me, Claude merely smiled. "Not a problem, Barry. OK if I join you?"

Whew! Dodged another bullet, I thought as I scurried to fetch him a drink. Naturally, I also refilled my own glass many times during the party and managed to get exquisitely hammered.

When I awoke the next morning, I recalled what we had done and realized how stupid we were. If Claude had complained to the brass, we could have been in shit. I shared my concern with Rick, but he just laughed it off. The way he figured it was once Claude joined us, there was nothing to worry about.

---

17   https://www.tvo.org/article/john-robarts-died-30-years-ago-today

AU REVOIR

On October 29, 1967, the curtain came down on Expo 67. I felt nostalgic as I bid farewell to my friends as they left the pavilion for the last time. I had received a memo from headquarters informing me that I was being transferred to Kitchener, but the transfer was delayed because the OPP was required to provide security while the pavilion was deconstructed, and Rick and I had volunteered for the job. It was a no-brainer. We watched the workers pack the iconic art and sculptures. A boring task indeed! Fortunately, we discovered a way to relieve the boredom.

When Rick was nosing around, he discovered a fishing rod left behind by the cleaning staff. I recalled watching the cleaners catching speckled trout on midnight shifts. So, Rick and I drowned some worms, and as luck would have it, we caught a dozen trout. After work, we returned to Habitat 67 (where we stayed for the duration), and Rick cleaned the catch while I made martinis with my special recipe: two fingers of vodka teased with a few drops of vermouth. We enjoyed the farewell dinner, reminiscing about the fantastic time we had had at the exposition. Sadly, my boozing buddy passed- away in 1983 following a prolonged and courageous battle with colon cancer. Rest in peace, Rick!

VISITING UNCLE JACK

After the assignment ended, I decided to visit Uncle Jack at OPP general headquarters (GHQ). During the drive, I thought about Uncle Jack and Aunt Rhea. They never had children and were devoted to their stable of racehorses, including Whitty's Ace and Whitty's Joker. I visited them in 1948 when I was five years old. Uncle Jack was the commander at the Brantford detachment, and they lived in an apartment above the detachment. Whenever I visited them, it was a thrill watching officers leaving the detachment in the shiny black-and-white cruisers. Much later when I joined the OPP, I visited them frequently in Mississauga. I enjoyed listening to Jack reminisce about his time on the force until he got drunk and hit the sack.

When I arrived at general headquarters, I was escorted to Jack's office by a security guard. As usual, he was impeccably dressed in a three-piece suit. After some small talk, he asked me to drive him to a tailor's shop on Yonge St.

At the time, Nate Salzburg was a prominent haberdasher in Toronto. Jack became acquainted with Nate because of their shared interest in horse racing. Once he learned

Nate was a tailor, Jack, being the consummate "clothes horse," frequently replenished his suits from Nate's "stable" of stylish fabrics.

While Jack and Nate discussed Jack's horse's (Whitty's Ace) leg injury, I wandered around the shop admiring the assortment of fabrics, which ranged from conservative to ostentatious. Eventually, Jack examined the assortment of bolts and selected a fabric with a blue sheen and a red pinstripe, which I thought looked appropriate for either a mob boss or a pimp. Nevertheless, I selected the same fabric. To this day, I don't know what or even if I was thinking when I selected the same fabric. He was a quasi-father figure to me, so perhaps choosing the same material was my way of identifying with him or perhaps ingratiating myself.

When we left Nate's, Jack suggested going to the Mohawk Racetrack and betting on a few ponies. We were having a drink, and Jack was in his horsey world focused on the racing form. After a few moments, he left the table and joined a couple of guys near us. They looked like they didn't have a pot to piss in, but I guess Jack thought they knew their stuff when it came to picking winners.

"My friends told me Torpedo Tuffy looks really good," he said when he returned. We emptied our wallets and bet on Torpedo Tuffy to win. In my opinion, the nag should have been called Torpedo Dud because, you guessed it, she finished dead last!

After the race, we returned to Toronto. Jack was staying at a hotel, and after a couple of drinks, we hit the sack. The next morning, I awoke hungover and discovered we had just enough money to order grapefruit for breakfast. After we ate, Jack went to work, and I put in time roaming around the tacky souvenir shops on Yonge Street. After a few hours, my hangover subsided, so I went to headquarters and caught Jack as he was going to the commissioner's lounge for coffee. He invited me to tag along, and I immediately spotted Commissioner Eric Silk having coffee with some officers. As Jack introduced me, I thought about the time I had answered the phone in the office at the Expo site, and the caller identified himself as "Commissioner Silk." I thought it was one of my cop buddies pranking me. "Yeah right," I replied. But after the caller assured me that he really was Commissioner Silk, I responded in the appropriate manner.

After we had coffee and a stilted conversation with the commissioner, we returned to Jack's office, and he asked me to drive him home. When we arrived at his residence, Rhea greeted us with a cheerful smile. After bidding them farewell, I drove to Kitchener and reflected on the impact that Jack's chronic drinking was probably having on Rhea and their marriage. Ironically, it never crossed my mind that, years later, I too would have relationship problems because of my out-of-control drinking.

On September 27, 1977, I was working at Mount Forest District Headquarters when I was advised that Jack had passed- away. I knew he had throat cancer. Still, hearing that he passed saddened me. An official police funeral was held for Uncle Jack, a fitting tribute for Assistant Commissioner John Leo Whitty, who served the people of Ontario from 1930 to 1977. Uncle Jack was a very memorable guy. Yes, he was an alcoholic, but he still managed to achieve the prestigious rank of assistant commissioner. I truly admired him. Rest in peace, Uncle Jack.

CHAPTER 4

KITCHENER: 1967-1980

*One certainty about
policing is the uncertainty*

– Barry Ruhl

AFTER EXPO 67 CLOSED, I was transferred to Kitchener. It's one of three cities in the "Golden Triangle," a few miles north of Highway 401, the busiest highway in North America.[18] The city's name was changed from Berlin to Kitchener in 1916 because of anti-German sentiment during World War I. The municipality has several industries, including Kaufman Rubber, Budd Automotive, and Arrow Shirts. The University of Waterloo, Wilfred Laurier University, and Conestoga College are also located in the area. The city hosts the second-largest Octoberfest festival in the world, attracting between 750,000–1,000,000 revelers annually.

The detachment's compliment included a staff sergeant, five corporals, and forty-four constables. It was responsible for North Dumfries, Wilmot, and Woolwich townships and a section of Highway 401. It was a much busier detachment than my previous postings. At any given moment, phones were ringing off the hook, officers were booking prisoners, complainants were lined up at the counter, and officers were rushing out the door, responding to calls. The intensity was contagious, and I was hooked!

---

18   https://oppositelock.kinja.com/the-busiest-highway-in-north-america-1559577839

Barry Ruhl

BINGING MY GRIEF

When I arrived in Kitchener, I needed a place to stay. Fortunately, my Uncle Bud (my father's brother) and Aunt Gladys invited me to stay with them. The day I moved in, we sat around the kitchen table reminiscing over drinks, and I learned a lot about the Ruhl family history. I also knew I was going to enjoy living with Bud and Gladys They were a warm, engaging couple, and I was looking forward to a prolonged relationship. Sadly, Gladys passed- away unexpectedly in 1970.

The night she died, we were having a wonderful dinner, including her special recipe of succulent spareribs and sauerkraut. Yum! After dinner, I grabbed a few hours of shuteye before reporting for the midnight shift. The corporal updated the platoon on the occurrences from the previous twenty-four hours, and then I headed to my designated zone. A short time later, I received a call from the communication (comm) centre that was unsettling. With no explanation, I was advised to return to my residence. What the hell was going on?

When I arrived, an unfamiliar vehicle was parked in the driveway. I raced up the steps and was met by Gladys's physician. With a somber expression, he informed me that she had had a massive heart attack and died. I was speechless. A few hours earlier, we had been enjoying a succulent meal, and now she was gone.

Apparently, Gladys and Bud had gone to bed shortly after I left for work. She wasn't feeling well, so Bud called their doctor. He treated Gladys for a chronic heart condition, and she was feeling better, so they went back to bed. However, a short time later, Gladys stopped breathing. Alarmed, Bud called the doctor again, but by the time he arrived, she was gone.

When I entered the living room, Bud was sitting on the sofa, sobbing. We sat together, and neither of us spoke. I asked the doctor to stay until I booked off. When I left the detachment and headed home, I recalled Gladys wishing me well and hoping I'd have a safe night. I never realized it at the time, but her death would trigger me to dive into a pool of booze that would take me weeks to crawl out of.

Following the funeral, I returned to a home bereft of Gladys's heartwarming exuberance. Unexpectedly, her death hit me like a Mack truck. I was agitated, depressed, and forlorn. I turned to my favorite therapist, "Dr. Booze," and entered a foggy state of persistent abject grief. I stockpiled an ample supply of booze and hunkered down. Instead of numbing my pain, Dr. Booze took me into the depths of depression. For those who have never been there, slipping into this dark place is like sliding down a sewer pipe and finding yourself in a black hole with no windows, feeling hopeless. Finally—and fortunately—I vomited blood. Fortunately? Yes!

Puking blood scared me so much that I called my doctor in a panic. With little sympathy, he advised that the frequent retching was caused by excessive alcohol consumption. I had ruptured the veins in my esophagus and tore fissures in my gastrointestinal tract. He suggested that I stop drinking and prescribed Librium[19] to ease the withdrawal symptoms.

I listened to the doctor's advice but had withdrawal symptoms. My clothes were occasionally soaked in sweat. I felt anxious, I had no appetite, and I couldn't sleep. Throughout the agonizing ordeal, Little Barry was urging, cajoling, and coaxing me to drink. You probably know how it goes, but just in case you don't, his entreaties went something like, "Go ahead, have a drink. You'll feel better" or "Just have one. Just have one beer. It's just a beer" or "This isn't worth it. You know you're going to drink again, so you might as well start now." Nevertheless, I resisted his taunts, and after two weeks, I returned to work. I explained to the detachment commander that I had had the "flu." He never said anything, but I wondered if he believed me.

My prolonged bender had another unintended consequence. Shortly after Aunt Gladys's funeral, Uncle Bud asked me to find another place to live. Initially, Little Barry was angry. However, I could see his reasoning. He had just lost his lifelong partner and was grieving, and I had gone on a bender. I'm sure it added to his stress. Instead of being there for him, I was carousing all night and puking my guts out in the bathroom. In addition, he was subjected to the pungent smell of cigarette smoke as I chain-smoked butts throughout the midnight hours.

SELF-REFLECTION

I'm sure you are wondering why I drank to excess after Gladys's funeral. Also, you might be asking why anyone would drink to the point of vomiting blood. I have wondered that myself, and it has taken me a long time to come up with a plausible explanation.

You see, Little Barry, always wants to get drunk, but he doesn't always get his way. So, Little Barry is constantly on the lookout for an opportunity to take control of my

---

19 Librium is an antianxiety medicine that is also used to treat alcohol withdrawal (http://www.drugs.com/comments/chlordiazepoxide/).

personality and binge drink. For that to happen, there needs to be a reason or an excuse that makes sense to "Big Barry," such that he will surrender control to Little Barry. When Gladys' died, I was emotionally wounded. I had grown to love her like a mom, and this was the excuse Little Barry needed to convince me that stockpiling alcohol and getting shit-faced, was the way to grieve. So, that is exactly what I did. At first, binging for Gladys made sense. But once Little Barry takes control, he doesn't give it up readily. A significant event is required. In this case, that event was vomiting blood. When that occurred, Little Barry realized he should stop drinking and see a doctor. Nevertheless, after the crisis was over, Little Barry wanted to get drunk again, and it was all I could do to hold him at bay while I recovered from the bender. Incredibly, once I recovered, Little Barry started drinking again, with the proviso that binging would never happen again, but would it?

THE TOPPLED TOWER OF BOOZE

Now that I was no longer welcome at Uncle Bud's, my friend Gary, an OPP cadet, suggested I move in with him. Gary lived in an apartment near the detachment. The digs had two bedrooms, a small kitchen with laundry tubs, and a bathroom. It wasn't palatial, but it was ideal for two bachelors.

When my girlfriend Pat visited the first time, she was somewhat displeased to discover the laundry tubs full of dirty dishes. Worse yet, when she entered the bathroom, she spotted more dirty dishes on the shower floor.

"Why are there dirty dishes in the shower?" she exclaimed upon exiting the bathroom. I offered a reasonable explanation, or so I thought.

"Because the laundry tubs won't hold all the dishes, so when the tubs are full, we leave them on the shower floor until it's time to wash them." I could tell she didn't get it.

Soon after I settled in, Gary and I discovered we had a mutual fondness for booze. So, we thought it would be a great idea to stockpile a significant stash. When we returned from the LCBO (Liquor Control Board of Ontario) store, we cracked open a bottle of rye and, feeling no pain, decided to build a bar. After creating the architectural masterpiece, we headed to a hotel to celebrate. Yikes! When we returned, we discovered the broken remnants of our toppled "tower" blanketing the floor. Incredibly, and much to our delight, a bottle of vodka survived. After picking up the "dead soldiers," we had a few drinks and agreed that our bar-building days were over.

IN THE LINE OF DUTY

For a brief period, I accompanied officers on patrol. They showed me the detachment boundaries, the locations of raucous hotels, the criminal haunts, and the outlaw motorcycle clubs. I was chomping at the bit to go it alone, and after a couple of weeks, it was go time!

I found one activity particularly productive. I checked the seedy motels and noted the licence plates of vehicles. Not surprisingly, some owners had criminal records, and outstanding warrants.

YOUR FAMILY WAS KILLED

During a day shift, I was patrolling in Woolwich Township when I was dispatched to St. Jacobs to notify Wayne Green* that his mother, father, and sister had been killed in an accident near Ottawa. How awful was that? I thought how dreadful it would be to hear that my entire family had been wiped out. I drove slowly, thinking of a sensitive way to deliver the devastating news, knowing it would irrevocably devastate Wayne's life.

I located the address and spotted a young man raking leaves and wearing a University of Waterloo jacket. After confirming his identity as Wayne Green, I broke the news. "Wayne, I'm very sorry, but I have some very tragic news." He stared intently at me as I tried to remain calm. "Your family was involved in an accident near Ottawa. Their vehicle was struck by an oncoming vehicle, and none of your family survived." As I spoke, he listened without commenting or exhibiting any significant emotional reactions. Clearly, he was struggling to make sense of what must have seemed to be incoherent information.

"I've lost everyone," he said after a few seconds in a barely audible voice. "They're all I have. I'm all alone."

My heart ached for him. However, there was nothing I could do to lessen the pain. I asked if anyone could stay with him until other relations arrived, and he mentioned his next-door neighbour. He was at home, and after I explained what happened, he accompanied me to Wayne's residence.

When Wayne saw his neighbor, he started to cry. I felt sad and helpless after leaving his residence. I kept thinking how unfair life could be. As a matter of fact, one of the greatest burdens that officers carry through their careers is the weight of experiencing directly and vicariously the misery visited upon some people. Sometimes bad things happen to good people, and it stinks.

Barry Ruhl

THE WINNER BY A NOSE

Dealing with violence, actual or threatened, is a task that is central to the police mission of maintaining law and order. In many situations, the violence is exacerbated by booze. After being on the job for a while, it was obvious that if it were not for booze, our duties would be somewhat lessened. The detachment covered many licenced premises, and to a large extent the disturbances at such places were minor. But that wasn't the case when I was dispatched to a fight at a hotel in Ayr, southwest of Kitchener.

When I arrived, two burly, bloodied combatants were rolling on the floor.

"Break it up!" I shouted. Thankfully, they stopped and stood up.

There are times when a situation screams "gallows humour," and this was one of them. When the brawlers looked at me, I saw the nose of one of the combatants hanging precariously by a thread. His face was covered with blood, so I didn't think he was aware that he had almost lost it. My inner voice was screaming, *Winner by a nose!*

When backup arrived, we separated the men. The injured combatant was taken to Galt Memorial Hospital, where doctors reattached his nose. A subsequent investigation revealed neither drunk could recall why the dustup had occurred. I charged the Mike Tyson wannabe with assault causing bodily harm. He pleaded guilty and was sentenced to six months in jail.

IT'S A SHITTY JOB

Sometimes police officers are assaulted. Regrettably, some are assaulted in shitty ways. My stinky story began when I was working midnights. I was guarding a prisoner arrested for assault.

In every unfortunate incident, one or two errors of omission contribute to unintended consequences. In this case, I assumed the prisoner had been searched. I also assumed he was handcuffed because his hands were behind his back. Wrong!

After the arresting officer left the room to get some paperwork, the prisoner grinned at me.

"What's so funny?" I asked, stepping toward him. Suddenly, his arm swung out from behind his back, and with "fecal fury," he struck me square in the face with a handful of shit! That's right! Unadulterated, stinking crap. I was stunned! For a split second, I wondered what the hell had just happened. When I finally realized what it was, I was seething with rage. After I regained my senses, I scraped the crap from my face and returned the favour! The prisoner fell backwards, and I gave him a "feces facial." I can hear some readers thinking police officers should maintain their composure. I call bullshit on that. There are times when passion overrides reason, and for me, this was one of those times

After I washed the crap off my face, I went home to change my uniform. Pat was sleeping, so I left the soiled shirt on the balcony. As an afterthought, I left a note advising her to avoid the balcony. I returned to the detachment and charged "Shit Face" with assault. When he appeared in court the next morning, the judge instructed the court officer to take him to the restroom to wash his face. Subsequently, he pleaded guilty and was sentenced to sixty days in jail.

WELCOME TO SAUBLE BEACH

In 1970, I was transferred to Sauble Beach for the summer. A picturesque resort town 25 km west of Owen Sound on the pristine shores of Lake Huron. It's a tranquil hamlet inhabited by 2,000 full-time residents. However, during the summer, it is invaded by thousands of transients, including families, entrepreneurs, and exuberant, unleashed teens. The residents tolerate the carnival atmosphere because the tourist dollars keep their taxes relatively low.

The detachment personnel included a sergeant, a corporal, and ten constables. The officers were seconded from detachments throughout the district and billeted at the Kit-Wat Motel on the south shore of Sauble River.

When I arrived at the motel, I met my partner, Paul Farroll, and we hit it off from the start. He was a great guy, someone I wanted watching my back. I also realized we resembled Oscar and Felix from the movie *The Odd Couple*. This was obvious when I watched Paul ironing his uniform. In true Felix fashion, he completed the task and then carefully hung it in the closet. I glanced at my discarded uniform hanging over the closet door and realized I was Oscar.

BEACH PATROL

We spent hours walking the beach and essentially making our presence known. The business section was always overflowing with tourists visiting the souvenir shops and munching on hot dogs, hamburgers, and fries smothered in gravy at the many fast-food concessions. To a large extent, the beach was relatively quiet during the day shift. However, when the sun set, a much different scenario emerged. The party animals vacated their nests, searching the dingy bars for prey. Barroom chatter and booze enhanced the excitement of the hunt. So, the hustlers and the hustled searched for that special someone. If they got lucky, they could watch the sunrise together.

TAKING CARE OF BUSINESS

One of our goals was to keep a lid on underage drinking. Essentially, we wanted everyone to enjoy themselves without the outlandish behaviour caused by drunken teens. So, when we spotted a group of teens on the beach, we paid them a visit.

"Hi guys," we'd say. "You wouldn't have any alcohol in the cooler, would you?" More times than not, the stammering response would be, "Uh, well…" as they looked at each other for something to say. If there was booze in the cooler, we presented them with two options. "OK, guys, the fine is one hundred and three dollars. Now, I could charge each of you with possession, but if one of you claims ownership, only that person will be charged." This usually worked, and often one of the miscreants would claim the booze. As we were leaving the party that was not to be, we got a thumbs-up from the grateful families nearby.

Paul and I were on the same page when it came to enforcement. We gave warnings for minor transgressions, such as possessing a partial bottle of beer. However, if we arrested inebriated teens, it had a different outcome because they were at a high risk of injuring themselves.

In one situation, Paul spotted an intoxicated teen staggering along the centre of the highway. He was impeding traffic and shouting obscenities at the drivers. We were about to arrest him when he took off. He wasn't difficult to chase down and arrest. During the brief trip to the detachment, we were subjected to the usual barrage of drunken rants. After we locked him up, I was completing the arrest report when I heard a loud banging sound. What the hell?

We rushed to the cell block and discovered our drunken "guest" had smashed the toilet tank. We subdued him and placed him in restraints. The next morning, he was a sorry sight, expressing remorse for his outlandish behaviour. Nevertheless, I issued him tickets for being drunk and for damaging the toilet. I wondered what, if anything, he told his parents.

BOOZING ON THE RIVER

The Kit-Wat motel was the ideal locale to chill after work. It was essentially nirvana for the inveterate boozer. After "serving and protecting" the tourists, I lost the uniform and chilled by the river with my cop buddies. I especially liked to work the day shift because it afforded me plenty of down time to drink. To a large extent, the "bar" never closed, and we *usually* behaved. However, there was an exception to the "ruhl."

Les*, my brother "-in-law," decided to try his luck fishing, but didn't know what the hell he was doing! His initial cast landed on a yacht moored at the dock.

"Nice cast, Captain Nemo!" the other guys shouted. Resolutely ignoring the ridicule, Les baited the hook for a second toss and almost snagged his finger. Pole in hand, he staggered onto the dock and, much to our surprise, the cast landed in the middle of the river. Again, the chorus pitched in. "Nice cast, Les! But where's the fishy?"

Les began reeling the line when, bam! It tightened, and the rod bowed. From my years of drowning worms, I knew these were telltale signs of *fish on!* Suddenly, a pissed-off rainbow trout broke the water's surface, attempting to lose the hook.

"I got one, I got one!" Les exclaimed, frantically reeling it in. The chorus was no longer razzing him. One of the guys grabbed a net and landed the fish, a five-pound rainbow trout! No more kidding! It was all hands-on deck. A bunch of drunken cops took turns screaming "Fish on!" and "Get the net!" We landed a batch of trout using mini marshmallows as bait.

Although it was 2:00 a.m., someone suggested having a fish fry. "Yes!" the chorus shouted. In retrospect, we should have iced the fish and called it a night, especially since I was scheduled to work on the day shift. But reason was overwhelmed by demon booze, and the fish fry was on.

We cleaned the catch in the restaurant kitchen. Take a second to visualize a bunch of drunks attempting to clean fish as they scattered fish guts and scales everywhere. When we finished eating, we cleaned up after ourselves, or so we thought. The staff was understandably upset. They had to clean the mess before guests arrived for breakfast.

In the morning, I was (thankfully) on desk duty when a very pissed-off cottager came in to complain about the disturbance on the river. I told him I thought it was probably some bikers renting a cottage, and I'd speak to them.

When I recall this drunken debauchery, I know our behaviour was self-centred and inconsiderate. We disturbed the guests, caused additional work for the staff, and probably disturbed more than one cottager. Nevertheless, at the time I never considered any of the indiscretions. So, while we curtailed our midnight exploits, the "tap" was never turned off.

A PREDATOR STALKS HIS PREY

I was completing a report on day shift when a woman came into the office complaining that someone had stolen $100 from her purse. She said she had placed the purse on the floor beside her when she went to bed and then discovered the money missing when she was buying groceries the next day. Intrigued, I accompanied her to the cottage and noted there were no signs of forcible entry. When I walked around the cottage, I noticed faint footprints under the bedroom window. I also learned the victim had left the window open. It appeared as if someone had removed the money without entering the cottage. This was a real mystery that began a lengthy investigation that I have documented in another book, *A Viable Suspect*.[20]

During the investigation, I befriended a local businessman and longtime resident. We discussed the theft, and I asked if he knew anyone who could be responsible. I was surprised with his immediate response. "You might want to look at Larry Talbot.* He was caught red-handed peeking in a window where a woman was undressing. I don't think he was charged because he was a teenager." He also mentioned that Talbot's neighbours often spotted him taking nocturnal walks. The information was interesting, and I wondered if Talbot could be the perpetrator.

I completed a background check and discovered Talbot was 41 years old, 5 feet 10, and weighed 170 lbs. He was a traveling salesman employed by an industrial plumbing firm in Toronto. He lived at the cottage with his family during the summer months and resided in Scarborough for the remainder of the year.

I wanted to catch a glimpse of him, so I drove past his cottage on several occasions at night and finally spotted him reading a newspaper in what appeared to be the kitchen. It was around 2:00 a.m., which confirmed Talbot was a night owl. I also spotted him several days later staring at a young couple who were lying at the beach. Paul and I met with the detachment commander, who gave us the green light to watch Talbot.

The following week, we hunkered down behind his cottage. Although the lights were on, we didn't see him. Suddenly, Paul began thrashing. "I think a snake just crawled over

---

20   Barry Ruhl, *A Viable Suspect* (Victoria, BC: Friesen Press, 2014).

my legs!" Although he was deadly serious, I found it very funny. Nevertheless, we decided to call it a night.

The following evening, we parked in a lane approximately 150 metres north of Talbot's cottage. It looked like he was going to be a no-show, and we were about to pack it in around 3:30 a.m. when I spotted a shadowy figure walking fast in our direction. When he was about thirty metres from the cruiser, Paul hit the headlights. Startled, Larry Talbot, who was clutching a long pole, ran into the bush. We lost him. However, we discovered a discarded mop handle, and we realized it could have been used to hook our victim's purse, steal the money, and return it to the bedroom.

We met with the detachment commander and considered our options vis-a-vis Talbot. If he was questioned, he'd probably admit walking in the lane and carrying the pole to protect himself. Consequently, we decided to continue monitoring his activities. There were no incidents for the remainder of summer that were consistent with Talbot's modus operandi. We reasoned that our intervention may have scared him off and wondered if he'd continue to act out. I got that answer the following season!

FROM PREDATOR TO PREY

I returned to Sauble the following year and wondered if I'd be chasing Talbot again. My answer came in the midnight hours of June 28, 1971. Even though I was billeted at the Kit-Wat Motel, I rented a cottage for Pat, my fiancée, who had recently arrived from a holiday in Spain. I invited some of my cop buddies over for a barbecue. We had a wonderful evening sipping wine, munching on steaks, and listening to music. One of the songs was Credence Clearwater Revival's "Looking Out My Back Door," which would take on a whole new meaning for Pat and me.

After the guests left, we went to bed. A short time later, I was awakened from a deep sleep by a loud noise. At first, I thought some of my buddies were playing a prank on us. However, as I stumbled out of bed stark naked and looking for the light switch, I nearly ran into a dark figure standing in the doorway. He was wearing a garish orange mask. I jumped back in alarm and noticed he was pointing a gun at me. Holy shit, this wasn't one of my buddies!

"What's up?" I said. The room was silent as the intruder stared at us. Then he backed into the living room and uttered a terrifying command: "Get the bride out here!"

"Leave her out of this!" I said.

Just then, Pat appeared in the bedroom doorway wearing a short, slinky nightgown. In a gruff voice the intruder ordered Pat to lift her nightgown.

"I don't think so," Pat replied in a timid, almost inaudible voice. He pointed the gun menacingly in her direction.

"Lift it or I'll shoot!"

Trembling, Pat began to raise her nightgown. Impatient, the intruder used the gun to indicate she should move faster. (As this was occurring, my rage was building to a boiling point.) "Come on, come on. That's it, that's it." He thrusted his hips, as if he were having sex.

Suddenly, he stopped and ordered Pat to get my wallet from the fireplace mantle. She was terrified but managed to retrieve it. My wallet had an OPP logo on it, and I didn't want the bandit knowing I was a cop. So, as Pat walked near me, I grabbed the wallet and threw it on the floor. The intruder ordered me to pick it up.

"No!" I replied. By then I was seething with rage.

He pointed the gun at me. "Pick it up, or I'll shoot!"

"I don't think you will," I said, glaring at him. He stared at me for a few seconds and then bolted out of the cottage, grabbing Pat's purse as he fled.

Without thinking, I ran out the door after him. I chased him along King Edward Drive, providing a surreal spectacle for anyone fortunate (or unfortunate) enough to see a naked man in pursuit of a masked man with a gun and carrying a purse!

When he saw I was gaining on him, he yelled, "Get back!" and fired a shot, striking me in the chest. I was too pumped to realize a BB had struck my chest. (The projectile penetrated my skin but didn't cause serious injuries.) I managed to grab his coat, and he swung around, striking me several times with the gun. I wrestled him to the ground and pummeled him until he surrendered.

"Let me go! Let me go!" he pleaded. "Don't call the cops!"

I ripped off his mask and realized it was Larry Talbot. "I'm a cop, Talbot, and you're under arrest!"

The following morning, the OPP Identification Unit arrived from Mount Forest District Headquarters. They photographed the crime scene, including a broken window on our back door. (Talbot smashed the window to gain entry, generating the loud noise that woke us up.) They also took photographs of a pail used to prop the door open, presumably to effect a hasty retreat, and the clothes Talbot was wearing, including a dirty old coat, work pants, running shoes, and leather gloves. The grotesque mask was made from an orange industrial cloth secured to his head with butcher cord. Talbot was also carrying four sets of hockey laces, a skeleton key, and a sharp hunting knife.

Pat (Elliott) Ruhl (Credit: Barry Ruhl)

His vehicle was located 0.3 kilometres from us at a cottage that was for sale. The keys were located on top of the right-front tire. (Talbot's cottage was a short distance from ours, so he had probably intended to kidnap Pat.) Talbot's street clothes, underwear, shoes, and wallet were in the back seat along with sandwiches. A wooden dildo was discovered in the trunk. With frightening certainty, this indicated that Talbot was well organized and had carefully planned the break-in. Thank God I was there!

POST-TRAUMATIC STRESS

I was concerned that Pat might be experiencing some PTSD symptoms,[21] so her doctor prescribed Librium to help her cope with anxiety. She stopped taking the drug because she was concerned that she might become dependent. However, she remained hypervigilant and

---

21 Symptom categories for PTSD: reliving the event, avoiding reminders of the event, physiological hyperarousal (e.g., sleeplessness, anxiety, jumpy) and a multitude of questions with no answers as per the *Diagnostic and Statistical Manual of Mental Disorders (DSM–4)*.

anxious. When alone, she would sense danger and overreact to every strange or ambiguous sight or sound. When I worked midnight shifts, she left the hallway light on to dispel the shadows. She lived in constant fear of "something bad" happening. When she vacationed at our secluded island outside of Huntsville, she took a friend. However, on one occasion, she chanced going with our son, Jeff, *and* a .22 rifle. It wasn't a relaxing interlude, and when she tried to sleep, Larry Talbot invaded her psyche. *Was he on the island?* She returned home the following day. I also recall on an eerily quiet night when Pat awakened me, yelling, "Barry, there's a man at the window!" I thought I was going to shit the bed! Larry Talbot lived in Gravenhurst, only an hour's drive from the island.

On September 21, 1971, Talbot appeared before Judge H. C. Mosser at the county court in Walkerton. He pled guilty to armed robbery and received a suspended sentence and was placed on probation for two years. He was also prohibited from possessing firearms and entering Sauble Beach for two years. Pat and I were incensed by the light sentence. This was the judge's submission.

> Mr. Talbot, I have had the opportunity to peruse the reports of Dr. Renton and to consider carefully the statements made by counsel and the character evidence of your friends, which is all very favourable. These people have travelled a long way to say many good things and yet when you consider what happened at Sauble Beach, it must be shattering for the people who live in the area to learn that something like this can happen to someone who is a very kindly person and a very model citizen. This makes sentencing very difficult. From Dr. Renton's report there is little likelihood of you repeating the act that took place at Sauble Beach and there is very little likelihood that anyone in the immediate vicinity of Sauble Beach is going to be imperiled if you are given a suspended sentence and a probationary period.[22]

Pat and I were convinced that Talbot would strike again, and we were right! On October 11, 1978, at around 10:00 p.m., a woman spotted a man staring at her through her bedroom window. She screamed, and he fled, but he was arrested on Second Avenue North. The items seized included a loaded pellet revolver, a knife, two silk stockings (probably used as a mask), a roll of tape, a pair of gloves, a black flashlight, pliers, bolt cutters, two adjustable

---

22 Ruhl, 2014.

wrenches, and Adidas running shoes painted black.[23] On May 15, 1979, Talbot pleaded guilty to possession of burglary tools and was sentenced to six months in prison.

SELF-REFLECTION

From the time I arrested Talbot for breaking into Pat's cottage, I became obsessed. Over the remainder of my career, I investigated him assiduously, and I believe there's a credible case that he was a person of interest in a number of unsolved murders of young women in Southwestern Ontario, including the murder of twelve-year-old Lynne Harper in Clinton in 1959. Consequently, I wrote a book entitled, *A Viable Suspect*, which documents the investigative steps I took to indict Talbot. The results of my relentless investigation prompted the OPP to schedule an interview with Talbot on September 14, 2008. Remarkably, and regrettably, Talbot died on September 8, 2008.

Unfortunately, along with the cottage break-in, Talbot also broke into my psyche, and no matter how hard I try, I cannot evict him. Occasionally, I still have dreams associated with the cottage invasion. For example, I was sleeping at our home in Midhurst, and I experienced a dreadful nightmare in which a masked man jumped out of a laundry basket, pointing a gun, and screaming something unintelligible. I know that my obsession with Talbot resulted in less time with my loved ones. However, I also know the investigation provided me with a relatively positive way of coping with my post-traumatic stress without the use of booze.

WHO'S GOING TO CHARGE US?

In September 1970, I was summoned to attend the magistrate's court in Southampton. The matter involved a subject charged with mischief that occurred on the civic holiday weekend. The accused had smashed the window in an unoccupied OPP cruiser. I had witnessed the infraction and arrested him. Incidentally, I witnessed the offence when I was driving Staff Sgt. Jack Barnes* and Corporal Ron Wild* to the Kit-Wat Motel. So, the crown attorney wanted all three of us to appear.

---

23   Ibid.

The day before the trial, we decided to travel to Southampton together. So, we bought a case of beer and hit the road. As I sipped a beer, I recalled cruising the back roads with my buddies, but now I was a cop!

When we arrived in Paisley, a small town, southeast of Southampton, we stopped for dinner at a mom-and-pop restaurant. A friendly waitress seated us. When we sat down, Jack pulled a bottle of wine from his jacket and set it on the table.

"Holy crap, Jack!" I exclaimed.

He laughed. "Who's going to charge us? We're the police." Ron laughed at Jack's dumb ass quip. I didn't find it amusing and was concerned the local constabulary would catch us quaffing wine. In any event, the waitress brought three glasses, and Jack filled them with the illegal hooch. Despite my concern, I nervously sipped the wine. Although I was enjoying my dinner, I occasionally glanced at the door, expecting to see the police. Remarkably, my higher-ranking companions were oblivious and got a kick out of watching me squirm.

When we left the restaurant, Jack suggested we visit Kay at Sauble Beach. Kay was a cop lover and the proprietor of a take-out restaurant that we frequented. To show our affection, we called her "Mom," and had an open invitation to slip into the kitchen for coffee anytime. When we arrived, she welcomed us with open arms. Many nightcaps later, we crashed at her place.

I awoke the next morning with a massive hangover and a frightening thought: I was appearing before Justice Otto Mc Clevis. He was a no-nonsense judge who scared me even when I was sober. As I stumbled into my clothes, I resorted to wishful thinking, hoping the accused would plead guilty, negating the need for my testimony. The alternative seemed unendurable: stinking of booze while testifying within a few feet of a judge.

Magistrate's court was held in the Southampton town hall. When we arrived, the courtroom was packed, an indication there were many cases on the docket. We sat near the front. When I glanced around, I spotted "our guy" speaking with a lawyer. *Shit*, I thought. *There's going to be a trial!* My panic meter shot up when I recognized the lawyer. He was from Owen Sound and reputed to be one of the best. I didn't want to face him! I had a pounding headache, my heart was racing, I felt nauseous, and I was exhausted from lack of sleep. It was fortunate I was wearing a jacket because my shirt was saturated with sweat.

At exactly 10:00 a.m., the court constable called the assembly to order, and stern-looking Otto Mc Clevis took the bench. He was impeccably dressed in a business suit adorned with a flower in the lapel. Court was in session, and I hoped the judge was in a good mood.

I had previously witnessed his sarcastic vitriol cast at witnesses who provoked him. I didn't want to be in his sights when it was my turn to testify.

Boy, could I use a drink, I thought. I knew a drink was waiting for me across the street. The Bucket was a local watering hole notorious for barroom brawls. However, it was going to be awhile before I could knock back a cold one.

Finally, our case was called. My heart was racing as the court reporter read the charge: "Steven Stone, you are charged that on the second day of July 1969, you did commit the crime of mischief contrary to the Criminal Code of Canada. To wit: damaging an OPP cruiser. How do you plead to the charge?"

Guilty, say guilty, was my wishful plea.

The accused stood silent for a moment and then uttered the only word I wanted to hear, "Guilty."

Thank you, thank you, thank you, I thought, exhaling with relief. He didn't have a criminal record, so he was given a stern lecture and placed on probation for two years. He was also required to reimburse the OPP for the broken window.

Recess was called, and I rushed to the Bucket with my boozing buddies to "drown" the hangover. When I entered the seedy hotel, I reveled in the pungent scent of stale beer and cigarette smoke. The décor was tired, but when I was looking for the hair of the dog, any "kennel" would do.

After I tossed back a couple of drafts, I was ready to head home, but Little Barry was just getting started! Consequently, our boozy trio downed several pitchers before hitting the road.

As we travelled through the desolate Bruce County countryside, Ron discovered the gas gauge was almost on empty. So, we three shit-for-brains searched frantically for a gas station and, luckily, found one near Walkerton. I fell asleep after we left, only awakening when Ron pulled into my driveway. I hit the sack immediately, not looking forward to the day shift.

I awoke feeling queasy after two days of boozing, and I was tempted to call in "sick." I listened to the rush-hour traffic on Highway 8, and for the first time in my career, I felt anxious. What the hell was going on? Usually, I was rushing to grab a black-and-white to chase the bad guys. Perhaps the two-day binge had affected me, even though I had never experienced free-floating anxiety following other binges. However, I stuffed my feelings and hours later, I was feeling better when I hit the road.

SELF-REFLECTION

When I think about that two-day binge, I realize how fortunate I was to have dodged many bullets, including Liquor License Act violations, being unfit for duty, and occupying a vehicle where the driver was impaired. (Not to mention Police Act violations, including conduct unbecoming and discreditable conduct.) I was walking along the edge of the precipice to oblivion. I think this reality was hitting home because after the binge, I wondered how much longer Lady Luck would be on my side.

TOGETHER FOREVER

During twelve years at Kitchener, I responded to a multitude of occurrences. In police parlance, an occurrence is just about any type of event that police officers encounter. Many occurrences tend to be mundane and minor in nature. They include barking dogs, neighborhood disputes, and landlord/tenant complaints. However, there were also serious occurrences, such as sexual assault, robberies, and accidental death investigations. For example, I vividly remember two young men drowning on the same day in the same lake. I still see the face of a woman who died in my arms after her vehicle struck a bridge. However, the occurrence that continues to haunt me was the tragic death of two young brothers, ages eight and six, in the village of Linwood.

Linwood is a hamlet in the northwestern section of Waterloo County. I was working days and dispatched to a shed fire at a residence there. When I arrived, the fire had been extinguished. I exited the cruiser and spotted a couple sitting on the back porch of the house. They appeared to be grief stricken. A large crowd was staring at a shed at the rear of the property.

I entered the shed cautiously, not knowing what to expect. When my eyes adjusted to the darkness, I was seized by the horrific sight of the charred remains of the two young boys lying on the floor. The older boy was lying on top of his younger brother. Based on their respective positions, it appeared the older boy had been attempting to protect his younger brother. (A report from the fire marshal indicated that a witness saw the boys playing with matches minutes before the fire department was alerted. Consequently, the fire marshal classified the cause of the fire as "misadventure.")

When it was time to remove the bodies, the firefighters formed two columns from the shed to the coroner's wagon. They also raised emergency blankets to shield the boys' bodies from inquisitive gazes. As I write this, I can still see the grief-stricken faces of the firefighters and bystanders. I believe everyone felt a profound connection to the boys. A tremendous sense of loss connected with our collective humanity.

Shortly after the bodies were removed, I was alone with the boys' parents. Grief stricken, the father asked if it was their boys. Even though it was their boys, I explained that their identities would require confirmation. I requested the name of their dentist. The parents never asked why I needed that information. (The dental records were required because the boys were burnt beyond recognition.)

The interview with the parents was heart wrenching. (It was always difficult to conduct interviews with grieving next-of-kin.) The father's hands shook as he puffed on a cigarette, and his wife sobbed uncontrollably as they recalled the last time, they saw their boys. When I completed the interview, I extended my condolences and bid them goodbye.

When I was returning to the detachment, I thought about the surreal image of the older brother shielding his sibling from the raging fire. A poignant symbol of brotherly love. They were bonded in life and now in death: together forever. When I reflect on the horrific death of the brothers, I feel a profound sadness and an emptiness that defies description.

On the anniversary of the boys' deaths, their mother called. In a barely audible voice, she said she had a dream that her boys had been murdered. I asked her to recount the dream. She related that the boys had been bound with rope before they were engulfed in the fire. I recalled a piece of rope was discovered atop the older boy's leg during the autopsy. However, it was the prevailing opinion that the rope fell from the rafters during the fire, and there wasn't anything nefarious about the boy's deaths. I shared the explanation with her, and she seemed to accept it. I still think about the boys and their parents. I should have visited them, but something always stopped me.

SELF-REFLECTION

The boys died on August 12, 1972. At that time, most officers had never even heard the word "stress," let alone the term "post-traumatic stress disorder." By that time, I had been on the job for eight years. I had seen other distressing things, but none of the calls bothered me to the extent that this one did. I wasn't able to get the image of the boys' bodies out of my head. I had trouble sleeping and concentrating, and I was not my fun-loving self. In my drinking days, I would have drunk myself into oblivion. Instead, I received the support I needed from Pat.

Fortunately for me, I married Pat in May 1972, three months prior to this occurrence. Pat asked about how the death of the boys affected me and listened without offering advice. Instead, of turning to the bottle, I turned to Pat to talk about my thoughts and feelings. Later in my career, I became a peer supporter and learned how dangerous and insidious post-traumatic stress can be.

Police officers are humans and are susceptible to the traumatic events that they encounter. But the macho male culture demands that officers, man up and suck it up even if the events cause emotional stress. This also applies to women, who buy into the "tough it out" culture when they become cops. Consequently, police officers and other first responders, including nurses, doctors, and fire-fighters stuff down their reactions to traumatic events and act as if they are OK. However, to maintain a façade, many police officers turn to the bottle to self-medicate. I was fortunate to have Pat, and she was exactly what I needed at the time. She didn't judge, she didn't question, and she didn't give advice. She listened and provided me with the support I needed to address my post-traumatic stress. Unlike Little Barry, Pat cared for me, and that feeling of being genuinely cared for was better than any bottle that Little Barry could offer.

SHE'S THE ONE FOR ME

I met Pat at Sauble Beach in 1969. Paul, my partner, invited me to tag along to a party at his fiancée's cottage, and Beth Shouldice introduced me to Pat. I enjoyed chatting with her but didn't think I'd see her again. However, the following year, Beth played Cupid, and we went on a double date to the local drive-in with Beth and Paul. That was the beginning of a wonderful relationship.

During the summer we had a blast partying at the motel and taking frequent trips to the beach. It wasn't long before she discovered my fondness for booze. I recall her saying she had never seen so much boozing until she met me. (Her mom and dad only drank on special occasions.) I remember walking by an officer's room at the Kit-Wat, and she spotted beer cases stacked floor to ceiling. She seemed surprised.

"Did he drink all that beer?" she asked.

"Not all of it," I replied. "I helped him."

Later, when she met Uncle Jack, she discovered that when the cap came off a bottle of booze, it didn't go back on! The heavy drinking bothered her to the extent that she mentioned it to her mother. "You better make sure you want to marry him," her mother said. "I have seen how alcohol can affect a family." She was referring to her alcoholic father.

Pat and I dated for two years before tying the knot. We enjoyed socializing with our friends, going to movies, cruising throughout the countryside, and attending parties. However, there was one party she didn't enjoy. On that occasion, I got drunk and became extremely argumentative, picking a fight with one of my cop buddies. Apparently, my actions escalated to the point that others intervened, claiming that I'd have to go through them to get to my buddy. The next day Pat was really upset, and with good reason.

In March 1971, Pat and I were dining at my favourite watering hole in Breslau. I asked her to hold out her hand. She extended it palm side up. "No, the other way," I said. Then I slid an engagement ring onto her finger. She was so excited that she called the waiter over and showed him the ring along with her gorgeous smile.

Later, when we were driving to Toronto, she periodically turned the interior light on and stared at it. We chose May 13, 1972, as our wedding date and were kept busy planning the special day. It seemed like everything was going as planned. Wrong!

It was on June 29, 1971, that Larry Talbot broke into Pat's cottage at Sauble Beach. The emotional aftermath was extremely upsetting for both of us. To add insult to injury, I was ordered to submit a report explaining what I was doing in a cottage with a single woman at 4:30 in the morning! Neither of us had experienced anything as violent as the cottage invasion. Nevertheless, we supported each other, which reinforced our devotion and love, and there weren't any repercussions from the brass for being with my fiancée at the cottage. (I even received a letter of commendation from Commissioner Eric Silk congratulating me for the courage I displayed arresting an armed intruder.)

May 13, 1972 was a beautiful spring day when we exchanged our vows at All Soul's Anglican Church in Willowdale. The reception was held at a beautiful golf club in Thornhill, and much to my delight, the "Red Ruhl Group" provided the music. (Regrettably, my father died two months after the wedding.) Following a fantastic honeymoon in Bermuda, we rented an apartment in a high-rise in Waterloo. It was on the seventeenth floor and afforded us a panoramic view of the countryside.

CHAPTER 5

SOBRIETY AND THE ROAD TO RECOVERY

> What is it about a beautiful afternoon
> with the birds singing and the wind rustling through the trees
> that makes you want to get drunk?
>
> – *Jack Handey*

PAT AND I WERE ENJOYING our lives together, but my excessive drinking was beginning to bother me, and I was seriously considering abstinence. Many alcoholics only quit when they hit "rock bottom," realizing their drinking is out of control. I was faced with this dilemma after visiting a cousin who lived in a cottage near Meaford. He couldn't attend the wedding, so we decided to visit him. He was delighted to see us and enjoyed hearing about our special day. It was a beautiful afternoon, so we sat on the patio overlooking Georgian Bay. I volunteered to fetch the drinks. Unfortunately, Little Barry was enticing me to "double up," so I knocked back double shots of vodka on the sly. Consequently, I was in the bag big time when we said goodbye.

While driving through Meaford, I decided to visit an old friend from when I was stationed there. Unfortunately, I don't have any recollection of the visit! I awoke at the Meaford General Hospital with an IV needle stuck in my arm, scared shit-less.

"What the hell happened?" I asked.

Pat, who was upset, related that after we arrived at my friend's home, he took us on a tour of his gardens, and I tumbled head over heels into his rose garden!

When I arrived at the ER via an ambulance, I was examined by Dr. Joe Wirkkunnen, who I had drank with occasionally when I was stationed at Meaford. He asked Pat how much I had to drink. "Hardly anything," she said. "Perhaps one or two drinks." He looked at her with an incredulous gaze. "This is Barry we're talking about," he said, "and one or two drinks wouldn't cause him to be lying there." Joe was spot on. I had managed to get shit-faced, and he was simply reinforcing the notion that my drinking was over the top. I found it difficult to look at Pat and it was only two weeks after our wedding!

The following morning, a doctor with a stern demeanor delivered a frightening prognosis: my blood-alcohol concentration (BAC) reading was in the lethal range. *Christ, I almost killed myself,* I thought. It felt like I had been coldcocked. The doctor's prognosis spoke volumes, and he suggested that I get help.

After he left, I thought about my intemperate lifestyle. I accepted the doctor's dire warning as a wake-up call. I could lose Pat, my career, and ultimately, my health. I mused that I was lucky to be above the ground and not under it! Nevertheless, I didn't quit. No, Little Barry still had his hooks in me, but I did cut back.

JUMPING ON THE WAGON

I had my last drink on October 27, 1973. I was attending my brother-in-law's birthday party at the Hook and Ladder Club in Toronto and ordered a double martini. Unlike other occasions, I felt the effects of the alcohol immediately. This surprised and frightened me because I erroneously thought the years of excessive drinking had caught up with me. I thought my liver was no longer able to metabolize the alcohol. So, out of the blue, I announced I was going "on the wagon." I still remember the response from my father-in-law. "You don't need to quit," he said. "Couldn't you just have a few drinks?"

"Bill," I explained "I know I'll feel better if I quit." (I never elaborated because I was ashamed to admit I was an alcoholic.)

I found it challenging, but I kept my pledge one day at a time. Everyone has unique experiences detoxifying. For several weeks I felt anxious, sweated profusely, and had occasional bouts of diarrhea. In addition, I suffered from lack of sleep. I also craved alcohol around the five o'clock cocktail hour. The cravings lasted for several months. Sometimes I would join my cop buddies barhopping, and it was agonizing watching them toss back the booze. Nevertheless, I was firm in my resolve. I remained sober for nine years and was physically and psychologically healthy. The years of awakening with hangovers and feelings of guilt and regret were gone. I was sober, and I embraced it one day at a time. Life was good.

TRADING BOOZE FOR SHOES

When I quit drinking, I traded booze for shoes. That is, I started running and gradually became quite proficient. What motivated me to start running? I looked in a mirror one day and realized I was getting fat. Initially, I began by walking. Then I progressed to jogging around the block. Because I had been sedentary for years, it was challenging. So, when I was out of breath, I walked until I recovered. After a few months, I was running instead of jogging. It felt exhilarating, and I was hooked! In fact, from 1973 to 1984, I ran 17 marathons, (26.2 miles), three 50-mile races, a 36-mile race, and many shorter races. On October 5, 1980, I completed my most challenging run. It occurred at Seagram Stadium at Wilfred Laurier University in Waterloo. I ran one hundred miles in nineteen hours and twenty-one minutes. I was elated when I finished the run, but I wasn't feeling well and was taken to Kitchener-Waterloo Hospital by ambulance. Visitors were restricted, so only Pat and my mother were allowed in the room. That is, until a couple of my running buddies showed up declaring they were my brothers. I was also visited by Dr. James Thompson, a professor at the Faculty of Human Kinetics and Leisure Studies at the University of Waterloo. He was interested in examining the aftereffects of the run, and I signed a consent form enabling him to obtain blood work. Several months later, I received a letter from Dr. Thompson informing me, …other than the tendon and lower leg problems, your run went very well physiologically and biochemically."

I realize now that I had simply replaced one addiction with another. Running became my drug of choice, but I didn't accept this notion during my running days. For me, it was simply running. I didn't realize the more I ran, the more endorphins were produced, resulting in euphoric feelings. The runner's high! A high that essentially mirrored the feeling I obtained from drinking. However, there are distinct differences between running and drinking. Running is physically, emotionally, socially, and spiritually healthier than drinking. Although there was a refractory or down period on some occasions when I ran, I didn't experience the dreaded hangovers. Running also afforded me a sense of achievement and serenity that I never obtained from drinking. Nevertheless, I was running excessively, and just like my drinking, it affected me physically, socially, and psychologically. In an article called "Know the Signs of Unhealthy Exercise Addiction," Richard Benvo writes,

> …there is a negative side to exercise that gradually insidiously can take over the positive…Exercise addiction, on the other hand, is a chronic loss

of perspective of the role of exercise in a full life. A healthy athlete and an exercise addict may share similar levels of training volume -- the difference is in the attitude. An addicted individual isn't able to see value in unrelated activities and pursues his sport even when it is against his best interest.[24]

Once running became my drug of choice, I became obsessed not only with running but also with maintaining meticulous diaries highlighting my toxic roller-coaster ride. I penned the highs and lows, including mood swings. I also documented the disagreements I had with Pat and my doctor, who attempted to discourage me from participating in the hundred-mile run. Running was of paramount importance to me no matter the season or the weather. I ran in the pounding rain, scorching heat, and blinding blizzards. There were days when running was glorious, and I was immersed in the sights, sounds, and smells of the surroundings. Unfortunately, Pat's recollections are different. She recalls preparing dinner and having to wait patiently until I returned from a run. When she voiced her displeasure, I reminded her that running was better than boozing. End of discussion. Now I realize that running, like boozing, had a detrimental effect on our marriage and compromised my health. Nevertheless, substituting shoes for booze probably saved my life. (I also managed to obtain two university degrees during that time that I never would have received if I continued to booze.)

END OF WATCH

On February 20, 1976, my supervisor, Cpl. Don Irwin, was murdered in Florida. Don had befriended a Florida state trooper named Phillip Black while vacationing in the Sunshine State and was accompanying his friend on patrol. When they checked a parked vehicle near Deerfield Beach north of Fort Lauderdale, they were shot to death. Walter Rhodes, Jessie Tafaro, and Sonia "Sunny" Jacobs were eventually captured and convicted of first-degree murder. Rhodes and Jacobs were sentenced to life in prison, and Tafaro was executed on May 4, 1990.

Don's death prompted me to consider my own mortality. I had never thought about being killed on the job, but that reality almost hit home during a midnight shift in the summer of 1976.

---

[24] https://www.active.com/articles/know-the-signs-of-unhealthy-exercise-addiction

I was dispatched to an armed robbery that had just occurred at a Shell station on Highway 8. The suspect was reportedly armed with a gun and last seen running toward Highway 401. I didn't see anyone as I passed the gas station. However, when I entered the eastbound lanes of the 401, I spotted a figure walking in an easterly direction. I also spotted a Waterloo Township Police cruiser about three hundred metres east of my location. I exited the cruiser and yelled at the individual to stop. He turned and approached me. I asked him where he was coming from.

"London," he replied. The guy was calm, and his story made sense, but I noticed his pants were wet. (I reasoned this could have occurred when he crossed the grassy median that was wet following a recent rain.) Intuition kicked in, and I asked him to show me some identification. He was about to reach into his pocket when the Waterloo cruiser roared up, and the officer threw the suspect against the cruiser yelling, "He's got a gun!" Following, a brief struggle, the bandit was handcuffed and searched. Much to my shock, we found a loaded 9 mm pistol in his pocket!

The Waterloo Township officer related that he had been checking a parked vehicle when the young occupant told him that his father was recently released from prison after serving six years for armed robbery and had just robbed a service station. Then he shared an ominous promise by his father. He vowed he'd never go to prison again! After the dust settled, I realized I owed my life to the bandit's son and the Waterloo Township officer. I could have met the same fate as Don Irwin.

TAKEDOWN ON HIGHWAY 401

On December 31, 1976, I was westbound on Highway 401 passing a slow-moving vehicle when I noticed neither the driver nor his passenger looked in my direction. I thought it was somewhat suspicious, so I requested a registration check, which resulted in a hit: "Subjects wanted for armed robbery—CIBC, Toronto branch. Use caution. Armed and consider dangerous." Bingo!

I requested a roadblock on Highway 401 and Sweaburg Road seven kilometres west of my location. I stayed ahead of the vehicle until I was four kilometres east of the roadblock. Then I slowed down, so the bandits would pass.

As we neared the roadblock, I felt a surge of adrenaline coursing through my body. *What if they know I'm following them and pull onto the shoulder?* I wondered. *What if they run the roadblock? What if they exit the vehicle with guns blazing?*

When we were two kilometres east of the roadblock, I advised the Woodstock officers to block the highway. We approached, and I spotted officers armed with shotguns shielding themselves behind their cruisers. Suddenly, the brake lights came on, and the bandits stopped. I activated the roof lights to stop the westbound traffic. An officer shouted for the suspects to exit the vehicle. Nada! He shouted again. Still no movement. I feared we were about to have a Wild West shootout. Suddenly, the doors swung open, and the bandits exited with their hands in the air. We searched them and then handcuffed them. I found $3,000 wrapped in a towel on the floor and two rifles and ski masks in the trunk. This was a successful takedown. No one was injured, two bad guys were arrested, and the bank got its money back. Funny how these things go. If they had waved or looked my way, they could still be on the run.

MENNONITES—THE DISTINCT MINORITY

Waterloo County is home to a large Mennonite population. They emigrated from Pennsylvania during the American Revolution, fleeing religious persecution. Mennonites are renowned for their farming expertise and propensity to help others. For example, following the tornadoes that devastated the Barrie and Grand Valley areas on May 31, 1985, hundreds of Mennonites flocked to the area to assist.

Mennonite – fall ploughing (Credit: Barry Ruhl)

There are several Mennonite sects in Waterloo County. The largest is the "horse and buggy" or Old Order Mennonites. They disapprove of technology and embrace faith, family, and farming. Regardless of inclement weather, their horse-drawn vehicles transport families to the meeting houses for services. Traditional attire for the men includes black hats, black pants, and blue shirts, and the women wear bonnets and dark dresses. Although most tourists maintain a respectful distance, some brazenly enter the meeting house property to get that "special" picture. They're a pain in the ass! One time I was completing a property check at a meeting house when I saw a notice on the door that said, "If you come to worship, enter. If you come to gawk, stay out."

I can count on one hand the times I responded to calls from the Mennonite community. However, one call will be forever etched in my psyche. I was dispatched to a farm north of Elmira where a person was reportedly injured. I assumed it was farm related. Boy, was I wrong!

As I drove down the driveway, I spotted a man running toward the cruiser, yelling, "Please come! My boy hurt himself!" I followed him into a barn where several people were gathered near a stall. They moved aside when they saw me, and I was stunned when I saw a young boy lying in a pool of blood! He had a gaping head wound, and I spotted a revolver beside him. I struggled trying to make sense of the bloody, surreal scene. It appeared the victim intended to kill himself. As we waited anxiously for the ambulance to arrive, the silence was deafening, interrupted by periodic moans from the family and the intermittent mooing of cows in the nearby stalls. It was heart wrenching to watch the family as they gazed at the ghastly head wound, the glistening pool of blood on the straw-covered floor, and the revolver lying beside the boy. The macabre tragedy left me saddened and speechless.

The ambulance arrived and transported the boy to the hospital. He died later that evening. From an investigative standpoint, it was easy to determine what had occurred. The boy had entered the barn knowing he'd be alone. From the position of the body, it appeared that he was sitting on the floor when he pulled the trigger. There was no evidence of foul play. So, in terms of the investigation, I was certain I knew how he had killed himself. Motivation was also established because he had been caught stealing a small sum of money. But where did he get the gun? I spent a considerable amount of time canvassing members of the community but came up empty. So, the investigation was an open-and-shut case. But I was troubled that he would take his life over something that seemed so minor, so insignificant. Why? He was a member of the Old Order sect where pacifism was practiced. Essentially, the sect was devoted to their faith, their families, and their farms. I tried to imagine what the boy was thinking before he pulled the trigger. What were his final thoughts? Was he overwhelmed by shame and fear of being shunned by his family and the community?

Based on my university studies, I now realize that people who commit suicide feel trapped in a triumvirate of despair. They feel helpless to change or improve a hopeless situation and, therefore, feel worthless. They genuinely believe that the world, their family, and everyone around them would be better off if they were dead. Their despair blinds them from seeing a workable solution or a positive outcome, so suicide makes the most sense. Whatever the boy was thinking, his profound despair probably blinded him to the fact that, as Christians, the Mennonite community was guided more by the principle of forgiveness than condemnation and punishment. There would have been consequences, but his indiscretion didn't call for the death penalty.

OUT OF THE BLUE AND INTO THE CIS

In 1978, I was assigned to the District 6 Criminal Investigation Squad (CIS). The unit was the brainchild of Det. Sgt. Don Westover responsible for supervising criminal investigations in the Mount Forest District. The officers were selected because of their acumen conducting investigations. They assisted detachments requiring additional expertise in major investigations. I was also selected to be the district intelligence coordinator (DIC).

The author working undercover
(Credit: Barry Ruhl)

I attended an intense three-week criminal intelligence course at the Canadian Police College in Ottawa. The curriculum included the skill set required to collect and disseminate intelligence information. I also attended rock concerts in the guise of an outlaw biker gathering intelligence. I was quite effective playing the role; however, I was naïve in terms of the drug culture. For example, I was working a three-day rock concert with other undercover operatives. We pitched our tents beside some party animals. One of them asked if I had any "papers."

"Uh, I've got the Globe and Mail," I said. I thought he wanted the paper to start a fire, not roll a joint! The guy just looked at me and then returned to his campsite shaking his head, probably thinking I was as dumb as a stump.

"SMOKEM" AT SAUBLE

On May 22, 1978, I was assigned to work at Sauble Beach for the long weekend. Prior to the holiday, a meeting was held for the undercover officers (UC) and the uniformed personnel, so the uniformed personnel would recognize us and understand what our role entailed. Essentially, we wandered around the beach targeting miscreants. If we spotted illegalities, we signaled to the uniformed officers by tugging on our earlobe.

During the weekend, one young fellow stashed his beer in the sand. After the uniforms confiscated it, I heard him mutter, "How the hell did the cops know my beer was there?"

On another occasion I was with a UC walking along the beach. We spotted two uniforms searching a vehicle.

"Hey, man, what's happening?" I said as we approached the vehicle.

"They're looking for our stash, but they'll never find it under the seat covers," the guy said.

"Cool!" was my hip reply. I walked by one of the officers and whispered, "Covers." Moments later, the officer emerged from the vehicle with a bag of grass. It was a small amount compared to the mountain of marijuana that would be smoked that weekend.

To a large extent, the UC assignment was relatively easy. For the most part, the kids were well behaved and happy to catch some rays after the bone-chilling winter. However, a campground from hell was located adjacent to County Road 21, eight kilometres north of Sauble Beach. It attracted the party animals, whose motto seemed to be "Get drunk, get stoned, get laid, and get in trouble with the cops."

The first sign of trouble occurred when a cruiser was pelted with beer bottles. My partner and I were operating an old clunker donated by a local dealership. When we arrived, I spotted a large crowd, and some of them were throwing bottles at passing vehicles while the unruly mob cheered them on. I realized this was dangerous and needed to be stopped. We were going to meet the brass at the detachment to strategize, but an officer at the scene requested we return because the mob was blocking the road, stopping vehicles.

We parked near the crowd and watched them for a few minutes. They were playing a game that I called "Smokem." It required a vehicle, a driver with a heavy foot, and revelers to lift the rear end of a vehicle, so the rear tires barely touched the pavement. On a signal from the lifters, the driver would rev the engine, creating a plume of smoke and the nauseating smell of burnt rubber. After a few seconds, the participants dropped the rear end, and the vehicle would take off, tires smoking.

One individual was not amused by these antics, the driver of an older-model Cadillac. He expressed his displeasure when the rowdy crowd surrounded his vehicle. The driver tolerated the throng for a few seconds and then suddenly exited the vehicle, shouting. "If any of you motherfuckers touch the car, I'll be back, and I won't be alone. You got it?" The outlaw biker patch he was wearing was an ominous sign that he wasn't kidding! Although the club frequented the beach, they never caused trouble, and I hoped that record would remain intact. The unruly crowd remained silent as they watched the burly biker leave. Once he was out of sight, the game resumed.

I mingled with the crowd, who were smoking dope and drinking, and I was pissed-off that we couldn't collar anyone because we were so outnumbered. Suddenly, a muscle car screeched to a halt, and it was obvious he was raring to play the game. I wanted a better look at the driver, so I sidled up to the car. He was all smiles as the mob egged him on and went into action. Some of them lifted the rear end, and he accelerated, causing the tires to smoke. Alarmingly large chunks of rubber flew off the tires, causing the drunken throng to move aside as the vehicle fishtailed down the road.

Although the behaviour was dangerous, there wasn't enough cops to confront the mob. A frustrating feeling indeed, but we wanted to nail one miscreant. So, we had a marked unit stand by north of our location. Suddenly a van rolled up to play the game, and the crowd went into action. After the "rubber hit the road," he was intercepted by the marked unit and arrested for dangerous driving. When we returned to the location, the mob had left.

The next morning, we searched for the muscle car on the beach strip. Luckily, we spotted it in front of a restaurant. I requested a marked unit and a tow truck to standby. We entered the restaurant and sat at a booth adjacent to the errant driver. He was bragging to a captive audience about his dangerous antics. After listening for a few minutes, I approached the booth and asked the stunt guy if he remembered me. "No," he replied tersely.

"That's OK," I said. "I'm Constable Barry Ruhl, and you're under arrest for dangerous driving." Mouth agape, he appeared to be stunned, and his bravado disappeared when I put the cuffs on him. He was taken to the detachment for processing. His muscle car was impounded, and we took photographs of the mangled tires. When he appeared in court, he pleaded guilty to dangerous driving and was assessed a fine and had his licence suspended. The judge commented that it was amazing no one was injured or killed, and he was right on!

FIRST RUNG ON THE "CORPORAL LADDER"

I entered the competition for the rank of corporal in 1978. My dream was to become a member of the elite Criminal Investigation Branch (CIB), and I needed to climb the corporate ladder to get there. The competition included a written examination and an interview. I was successful in the written exam and was scheduled to appear before the board, which included a superintendent, two inspectors, a sergeant major, and two staff sergeants.

The board was convened at District 6 headquarters in Mount Forest. I went for a run on the day of the interview because it helped me relax, but I still felt anxious when I entered the room and saw the five officers who would determine my destiny. As I began answering their questions though, my anxiety faded. The questions involved situations that a non-commissioned officer (NCO) might encounter during a tour of duty. I had spent many hours preparing for the interview, and none of the questions were problematic until the superintendent asked the following: "Okay, Constable you're off duty and receive a call at 2:00 a.m. from the dispatcher at the communications centre. He informs you that a motorist discovered a vehicle in the ditch, and the driver appears to be drunk. The registration reveals the vehicle is registered to me (i.e., the superintendent). What would you do?"

Under pressure I thought, *investigate or avoid? What response is he looking for?*

"Well," I began, "I'd contact the chief at Mount Forest and request an officer from that department investigate. I'd also notify the duty officer at general headquarters." Was that what they wanted to hear? The superintendent smiled. "Well, I don't think I want to be drinking and driving on Ruhl's watch."

Although the interview seemed to fly by, the time waiting for the results did not. While I waited, two questions swirled around in my head. First and foremost, was I successful? Second, if the answer to the first question was "yes," where would I be posted? If I listened to the rumour mill, the consensus seemed to be that I was going to be transferred to the District 7 Crime Unit in Barrie. I was ecstatic thinking that I might be going to a crime unit. Many officers sought such a position. Essentially the successful candidate would be responsible for the supervision of major criminal investigations within District 7. Again, according to the rumour mill, I was favoured because of my experience with the 6 District Criminal Investigation Squad (CIS). Apparently, the command staff had considered putting a CIS in District 7, and my expertise made me the frontrunner.

Finally, I received notification that I had been promoted and transferred to the District 7 Crime Squad. Bingo, my dream job! Pat and I were relieved and thrilled by the good news. Nevertheless, I was somewhat anxious thinking about the daunting challenges that awaited me in the new posting. Clearly, the brass was expecting me to implement a crime squad in the district. Although I was confident that I could undertake the initiative, I had misgivings regarding the detachment commanders' willingness to support the program. Often, new programs were met with passive resistance.

On a personal note, Pat and I were enjoying married life. We were the proud parents of a little red-headed boy named Jeffrey. I also realized and exulted in the fact that my ongoing sobriety was contributing to my success. But that success was soon to be cast aside when Larry Talbot "followed" us to Barrie and in the ensuing years caused me significant grief.

CHAPTER 6

THE BARRIE DISTRICT CRIME UNIT

ON JUNE 11, 1979, I reported for duty at Barrie district headquarters on Rose Street adjacent to the heavily travelled Highway 400. I felt anxious when I entered the imposing building. I was meeting Superintendent (Supt.) Roy Burkett, Commander of District 7. Although he had been my detachment commander (det. com.) in Kitchener, I was still nervous. Coincidentally, his first posting was at the Brantford detachment when Uncle Jack was the detachment commander. We briefly discussed the "good old days." Then he was all business and advised I'd be working with the detective sergeant (d/sgt.) to oversee major criminal investigations. I'd also be responsible for implementing a Criminal Investigation Squad (CIS). I was raring to go.

Before I left the meeting, Supt. Burkett asked why he needed the CIS in his district. His question surprised me and stopped me in my tracks. I had heard through the grapevine that he supported the program. I explained that the CIS would provide additional officers and expertise for detachments investigating major crimes. He seemed pessimistic and suggested that if the detachment commanders didn't get on board, the program wouldn't get off the ground. Even though I appreciated his concern, I assured him I would do my best to roll out the program. He simply nodded.

Following the meeting I arranged my personal effects in the crime unit. My supervisor, Detective Sgt. Ronald Rodgers,* was on annual leave so I became the acting detective sergeant. When he returned to work, I was in for quite a shock!

Meanwhile, I began organizing the CIS program. I received a boost when Supt. Burkett distributed my proposal to the detachment commanders. He wrote: "Corporal Ruhl's report reflects exactly what is required of the CIS Squad and its function in this District." He instructed Insp. W.A. Coxworth to ensure the directive was conveyed to the detachment commanders, and all but one supported the initiative. The holdout believed the program would adversely affect his detachment if even one officer was seconded to the CIS. Undeterred, I arranged a meeting with the "doubting Thomas."

I vividly recall the plume of smoke emanating from the chain-smoking commander. Although he listened, he responded with a series of "what ifs." Nevertheless, I managed to address his concerns. For example, I suggested that if there was a spike in drug or criminal activity, the CIS could assist the detachment with unlimited resources. This seemed to satisfy him, and he assured me that he would support the program.

A FAILURE TO COMMUNICATE—NOT! PROJECT SPIKE

The CIS had an opportunity to cut its teeth when we executed a project in the Midland area. The Midland detachment was experiencing a rapid spike in criminal occurrences. I met with Bill Boyd, the detachment commander, who presented a feasible argument for an undercover operation. The brass gave us the green light, and Project Spike was launched.

Contrary to OPP regulations, CIS officers wore beards and long hair. These changes helped them to infiltrate the criminal element. In a short time, the members were successful. Project Spike resulted in several arrests and the seizure of a large quantity of stolen property, weapons, and drugs. The superintendent was pleased with the results. The successful outcome was essentially the springboard that launched other projects in the district. Nevertheless, I soon discovered one person had hostile misgivings about my activities. You may recall my supervisor, D/Sgt. Rodgers, was on annual leave. During his absence, the Midland project was initiated and concluded. He knew nothing about it. On the morning he returned, Supt. Burkett had his weekly meeting with the detachment commanders to apprise them of the previous week's activities throughout the district. When the meeting concluded, I requested a private meeting with Supt. Burkett and Insp. Coxworth to update them on the results of the Midland project.

When I returned to the office, D/Sgt. Rodgers seemed angry. "Follow me," he barked. I followed him into the lunchroom. He slammed the door and then turned to me. "Who do you think you are asking for a private meeting with the superintendent and not telling me what the hell you've been doing?" His rant was accentuated by a shaking finger and spewing spittle. "You don't do anything until you talk to me!" With that injunction, I had had enough. The bullying tactics didn't intimidate me.

"Keep your finger to yourself," I said. Even though I was upset, I managed to adopt a façade of calm. "Insp. Coxworth instructed me to manage the Midland project on a need-to-know basis." This meant only officers involved were privy to the operation. Confidentiality was required because, unfortunately, some cops were prone to letting the cat out of the bag. Upon hearing the explanation, D/Sgt. Rodgers stomped out of the room and into Insp. Coxworth's office.

When he returned to his desk without speaking, I found his silence unsettling because I wanted to discuss the CIS program with him. The passive silence continued for days, so I decided to speak to Insp. Coxworth. However, Pat suggested I wait a little longer. I'm glad I did. Supt. Burkett met with us to plan the civic weekend at Wasaga Beach. Fortunately, following that meeting, he communicated with me. However, when I eventually received my annual performance evaluation, it was patently obvious that he continued to hold a grudge!

THE CIVIC WEEKEND AT WASAGA BEACH

I was looking forward to the civic weekend at Wasaga Beach. The resort is located on the shores of Georgian Bay approximately 133 kilometres northwest of Toronto. Over two million people visited the beach annually, including some miscreants. The troublemakers included outlaw bikers and rowdy youth who partied hard and kept us busy. We were fortunate to have Terry Hall on board. He was a member of the OPP Bike Gang Enforcement Unit and was masterful at infiltrating biker gangs. Regrettably, Terry died recently. Peter Edwards wrote about his passing in the *Toronto Star*.[25]

I selected eight CIS officers to mingle with the crowd. When they spotted violations, they would tug their earlobe to alert the uniformed officers. It was effective in terms of seizing liquor and drugs. I assumed the guise of a biker and roamed the beachfront looking for nefarious activity. Regrettably, I "burned" my cover when I was walking through a parking lot and spotted a couple of potheads smoking a joint. Rather than using the "tug" signal, I alerted a nearby officer by pointing at them. When the officer approached, one of them yelled, "I know what the fuck you're doing. You're a cop."

On Saturday evening I witnessed a violent assault outside a bar. A biker was putting the boots to a young guy cowering on the ground. He was beating the shit out of him, so I radioed for backup. The biker took off, and I followed him until the uniforms appeared.

---

25   https://www.thestar.com/news/crime/2016/01/04/terry-hall-led-police-campaigns-against-outlaw-bikers.html

When he spotted them, he took off running again, but the officers wrestled him to the ground, and he was handcuffed. I discovered he was a "prospect[26]" in a biker gang, and the assault was apparently his ticket to becoming a full-patch member.

Compared to other years, the weekend was relatively quiet. The deployment of Terry Hall's Biker Enforcement Unit and the CIS played a major role in keeping a thumb on the party animals.

When I returned to the office following the weekend, D/Sgt. Rodgers never mentioned the weekend, and I wondered why. We attended the superintendent's weekly meeting, where I presented the weekend stats and commended the officers for their efforts seizing an impressive amount of liquor and drugs. When I was finished, Supt. Burkett thanked me. In the absence of any sign to the contrary, I interpreted that to mean the CIS had done a commendable job.

SELF-REFLECTION

During my time at Sauble Beach, I drank almost every day. On many occasions, the drinking was excessive. When I say "excessive," I mean, I binged to the point of waking up soaked in urine. This was not only embarrassing, it was also quite injurious to my relationship with my friends, the motel owners. Now that I was sober, my experience at Wasaga Beach was much different. Because I no longer drank, I relished in feelings of serenity. Nevertheless, maintaining my sobriety was a twenty-four-hour-a-day challenge. Even though my commitment to remaining abstinent was absolute, I could never let my guard down.

After I quit, I was uncomfortable around drunks. I think my disdain served as a mirror of my own drunken behaviour. Periodically, a copper in his cups would ask why I didn't drink, which caused my blood to boil! Also, and equally important, I had to constantly fend off Little Barry, who was nudging me to have a drink. Little Barry is insidious and manipulative. He usually speaks when I'm around folks who are drinking. He says things like, "It's OK, Barry, one drink won't cause you to relapse" or "How can cops trust you if you won't drink with them?" or "Come on, have some fun, just one drink. You know you want it." Whenever I partied with officers, I was particularly vulnerable to Little Barry's pleadings

---

26   https://www.vocativ.com/underworld/crime/how-to-join-an-outlaw-biker-gang/index.html

and thus falling off the wagon and into the bottle. So, if the partiers were getting pissed, I'd head to the Georgian Bay shoreline where the serenity was intoxicating and go for a run.

PROJECT ANGUS

The village of Angus is situated adjacent to Canadian Forces Base (CFB) Borden, approximately twenty kilometres west of Barrie. The base is responsible for training approximately 15,000 personnel annually. We learned through a reliable informant that firearms were being stolen from the base by two bandits from Angus. Consequently, Project Angus was launched utilizing undercover officers (UCs).

One component of paramount importance in an undercover operation is the cover story for the operatives. The façade is meant to convince the targets that their new acquaintances (the UCs) are "bad guys." So, we needed to convince the targets that our UCs were wanted by the Calgary police. To authenticate the ruse, I had a buddy on the Calgary Police Service send me court documents from the Calgary court system. They included summonses ordering the "criminals" to appear in court for possession of stolen property. We also put Alberta plates on an old clunker donated by a local dealership.

With the scheme ready to get off the ground, our "bandits" met the informant at a seedy bar in Barrie to finalize the details and decide how the informant and the "bandits" knew each other. When they were comfortable with the cover story, the informant introduced the UCs to the targets. They hung around the bars in Angus buying them drinks and bragging about their criminal exploits out west. But the targets didn't reciprocate and were tight lipped about their nefarious activities.

An undercover operation is analogous to fishing. Sometimes we got a hit, and sometimes we got skunked. The "fish," weren't biting, so I put more enticing bait on the hook. I included "Pauli," another UC who was supposedly a mob guy from Toronto. He was interested in expanding his drug business in the Barrie area and was looking for help.

When Pauli picked up the 1976 four-door Caddy that we had acquired for the sting, he looked like a mob guy wearing a black three-piece suit, black shirt, and a thick gold chain around his neck. If anyone could pull the guise off, it was Pauli.

Once again, we threw out the line, and this time we got a hit! Our targets were sucked in by the "mobster," and he scored a large cache of stolen property. Pauli also attempted to acquire the stolen firearms, but it was a no go. So, we decided to cut our losses and go with what we had. The project was successful, culminating in the arrest of several individuals and the recovery of a large quantity of stolen property.

CONFLICT IN THE CRIME UNIT

I had been in the unit for a year, and it was gratifying that the brass seemed pleased with the CIS. However, it was a different story with D/Sgt. Rodgers. He never mentioned the squad. However, on my one-year anniversary, he handed me my annual performance evaluation and ordered me to sign it. I reviewed the evaluation, which included our initial conflict. He wrote, "[He]…must start consulting the D/Sgt. for advice and ideas before putting forth any activities to the senior District members for approval and implementation; must keep D/Sgt. advised of results first and to at least as great a degree if not greater than senior District members. Must follow chain of command." I was pissed-off! The comments were inaccurate and self-serving. I told him it was bullshit and I was going to submit a rebuttal. From that point forward, he stopped speaking to me unless forced to do so in terms of ongoing investigations.

The rebuttal included the following: I was instructed by Supt. Burkett and Insp. Coxworth to report *only* to them because they were concerned that any leaks would jeopardize the project. Second, D/Sgt. Rodgers never shared all the duties and responsibilities related to the d/sgt. position. I should have been apprised of them in the event the d/sgt. was absent.

I submitted the rebuttals. However, as soon as the report left my hands, I knew D/Sgt. Rodgers would be upset. I shared my concern with Pat, who listened intently. "What if you signed off on the evaluation essentially agreeing with Detective Sergeant Rodgers' allegations?" she asked. This was an excellent question. Indeed, if I signed off, I would be agreeing that my performance was flawed, and evaluations were maintained in an officer's personnel file ad infinitum. Pat's question justified my pushback, and I was confident I had done the right thing.

POETIC JUSTICE

Shortly afterwards, D/Sgt. Rodgers approached my desk. "Insp. Coxworth wants to see us," he said in a gruff voice. Once we were seated, the inspector read my rebuttal and then asked Rodgers to respond. He replied that he was my supervisor and should have been advised of the Midland project. Insp. Coxworth asked for my input. I reminded him that he and Supt. Burkett had instructed me to only share the project's information with the officers involved. I also mentioned that I'd been in the crime unit for a year, and D/Sgt. Rodgers had never discussed his "key task categories." Insp. Coxworth asked Rodgers if that was correct, and he replied in the affirmative. When the meeting concluded, Coxworth said he'd contact us in due course. As we left his office, I knew my relationship with D/Sgt. Rogers was going south bigtime!

Within a couple of weeks, I received a copy of the inspector's report. He accepted my version and instructed D/Sgt. Rodgers to bring me up to speed on his responsibilities. He also reaffirmed the instructions that I had received regarding the Midland project and essentially informed D/Sgt. Rodgers that I was following orders. Naively, I hoped the report would clear the air, but D/Sgt. Rodgers continued to ignore me unless there was a need to discuss ongoing investigations. Eventually, he was replaced by Barry Browning from Orillia. When we met, he related that he had "a lot to learn," and I reassured him that I would assist in any way I could. It didn't take long to realize we were very different. D/Sgt. Browning was quiet while I loved to talk. He wasn't into physical fitness while I was a member of the OPP running team. The most obvious difference was his propensity to smoke, and I was the recipient of the noxious fumes!

PROJECT SCAM

The Bracebridge detachment commander requested our help because there was a significant increase in drug trafficking in the detachment area. I met with a Bracebridge officer assigned to the investigation who was frustrated because he had contacted the provincial drug squad for assistance, and they kept putting him off. He was hoping the CIS could assist. I was eager to help, but we needed to jump through some hoops before getting a thumbs-up for an undercover project. I reviewed the officer's submission and believed an undercover project could be successful. I submitted a request for approval and got the green light. (I think our successful track record may have been the catalyst.) The investigation was called Project SCAM (Seize Cocaine and Marijuana).

This was the first time a detachment would take the lead in a major drug investigation. Essentially, I was responsible for monitoring the project's progress. Bracebridge was the epicenter, but as the project progressed, officers from Waterloo-Region, Metro Toronto, Halton Regional Police, and Edmonton became involved.

We got lucky when a wiretap revealed the chef at the Riverdale Inn* was purchasing cocaine. The project coordinator asked me to develop a ruse to enable an undercover operative to buy drugs from the chef. The challenge was to create a credible cover story.

I contacted the owner of a dry-cleaning business in Waterloo. He was also an OPP auxiliary officer and eager to assist. I concocted a cover story involving a fictitious individual named Phil Douglas. According to the ruse, Douglas had been employed by the dry cleaner but quit, and he was seeking employment in the Bracebridge area. The final piece of deception fell into place when the Riverdale Inn agreed to hire Douglas to work in the kitchen. It was showtime.

"Douglas" was an experienced undercover operative who gradually gained the chef's trust. He scored points when he complimented the chef on his culinary skills. The chef appreciated the plaudit, and before long they were barhopping. Nevertheless, Douglas was cautious and simply mentioned that he liked to "toke" or smoke "MJ."

The chef was noncommittal, so we had to up our game. We decided Douglas would simply ask the chef flat-out if he knew where he could score some coke. This tactic seemed risky. However, it was time to shit or get off the pot.

Douglas invited the chef to a bar for a few drinks. As the chef was getting pissed, Douglas told the chef he was hooked on coke and wondered if he knew where he could score some. Although he had a gut full of booze, the chef was tight-lipped. This was particularly perplexing since he had been overheard ordering coke on a wiretap. We wondered if the chef was suspicious of Douglas or didn't want to be the middleman in a drug deal.

Once again, we returned to the drawing board. This time I thought of something that might be a slam dunk. According to Douglas, the chef talked incessantly about visiting Toronto to watch strippers. So, we concocted a sting whereby Douglas would introduce the chef to his "friend" from Toronto who happened to be a stripper. I knew an officer who could pull it off, and the officer's supervisor approved of the proposal.

She met with the team and was given the cover name "Rosie." She also met with Douglas to ensure they had their stories straight in terms of how they were acquainted. Finally, she was briefed on the target's penchant for strippers. We devised a scheme in which Douglas would introduce the chef to Rosie at a bar. As the evening progressed, Douglas would ask Rosie where she was working. This would be her cue to introduce herself as a stripper.

After everyone was chilling, Douglas asked Rosie about her employment. She said she was working as a stripper at a nightclub in Toronto. To make the bait more enticing, she described some of her more erotic moves. Hooked! The chef was fixated on Rosie, all but ignoring Douglas.

After last call, it was time to reel in the fish. The chef slipped Douglas a baggie of cocaine. Now we had to unravel the web of deceit and dump the horny chef. They left the bar, and Rosie hugged the chef, promising to look him up the next time she visited Douglas. That parting gesture didn't satisfy the chef. He asked for her phone number, but she outfoxed him, explaining that she was shacked up with a guy and didn't want him to suspect she was fooling around. That explanation seemed to satisfy him. Consequently, the chef's obsession with Rosie was the catalyst that opened the floodgates, resulting in a successful project.

On November 15, 1980, the curtain came down on Project SCAM. Predawn raids were conducted in seventeen locations in Ontario and Alberta. Twenty drug-related charges were laid following seizures of cocaine, marijuana, hash oil, LSD, and barbiturates. Additionally, because of information received through Project SCAM, the Toronto Police Service seized a quantity of heroin valued at slightly less than $1 million. At the conclusion of the project, Commissioner H. H. Graham commended the officers involved …for their tenacity and professionalism in an undercover investigation of drug offences being committed in the Bracebridge area." I was pleased that Commissioner Graham had recognized the diligent work of the district members. I was also pleased that the brass had given us the thumbs-up to initiate Project SCAM. As a result, doors were opened for future drug-related projects in the district.

DROWNING MY SHOES IN BOOZE

In 1980, I learned that the International Police Olympics was going to be staged in Austin, Texas, in 1982. When I heard the news, I was excited, thinking I could compete in the games. I set my sights on the 10,000-metre, 5,000-metre, and half marathon. I had two years to prepare, so the training regime was intense. I ran sixty miles a week, incorporating ten sets of "fartlek" intervals to enhance my endurance: fast sprints, walking briefly, and then repeating the process. The technique elevated my VO2 max (maximum oxygen uptake.) I also included lung- busting hill sprints to the extent that I thought my lungs would explode! The tenacious training paid off, and I was in terrific shape. I was also grateful for the financial support when the OPP association and my running club paid for the trip.

I arrived in Austin on August 5, 1983. The temperature was 90°F, and I wondered if it would adversely affect my performance. I met my Canadian teammates from the RCMP and York Regional Police at the University of Texas, and then we marched into the stadium with athletes from around the world. It was exciting because I was about to discover if my intense training would pay off.

ON YOUR MARK

Before the start of the 10,000-metre competition, an official instructed us to raise our hands if we wanted to be sprayed with water. (The temperature was 98°F at 10 p.m.) I was registered in the master's competition for runners over forty years of age. I checked the competition and spotted a runner from the Australian team who I learned had been a previous member of Australia's Olympic track team. Yikes! I was about to run 25 times around a 400-metre track in 98°F heat competing against a former Olympian! But I was ready to challenge him. I had to relax, breathe easily, drink water, and maintain a comfortable pace.

The International Police Olympics – Austin Texas
(Credit: Barry Ruhl)

When the marshal fired the starter's pistol, I tucked in behind the Aussie. My plan was to follow him until the last couple of laps and then blast by him.

It was not to be. It was a lung-busting race, and although I tried a couple of times, he simply stepped up his pace. I had nothing left in the tank, and as we neared the finish line, I accepted that the Aussie was the better runner. But I gave it my best and crossed the finish line in second place. Even though I was exhausted, I felt fantastic! I finished in a time of thirty-seven minutes, eleven seconds. A personal best!

I was cooling down when the affable Aussie extended his congratulations and then handed me a beer. I was so caught up in the moment that I quaffed it without thinking. I had been on the wagon for almost eight years. After drinking it I told myself, "That's it, no more." But Little Barry had other plans. Instead of stopping, I drank well into the night with my teammates. We ran out of beer, so I gave a Mountie five dollars for a twenty-four pack.

"Hey, buddy," he said, "when's the last time you bought a case of beer?"

When I returned to my room, I had the presence of mind to affix my race number to my singlet for the half marathon in the morning.

I awoke on race day in no shape to greet the day with gusto. I reluctantly rolled out of the sack and splashed water on my face, but that did nothing to alleviate my pounding headache. I slowly donned my racing gear, dreading the thought of running thirteen grueling miles on a hot day. *Hmm…Maybe I could feign an illness. Why the hell did I get pissed?*

As the team drove to the stadium, I tried to think of an excuse to drop out. But if I did, I knew I'd be letting the team down, so I told myself to suck it up and go.

I lined up with the other competitors. When the gun signaled the start, I dropped to the back of the pack. I lumbered on mile after agonizing mile listening to Little Barry enticing me to quit. I was disgusted with myself for relapsing. In a sense I deserved the torturous trek for the lapse in judgment. I kept asking myself why I had thrown away the serenity that I had cherished for so many years. What was I thinking? No acceptable answer was forthcoming.

SELF-REFLECTION

Now in my role as an addiction counsellor, I realize times like these are when an alcoholic is vulnerable. In this instance, feeling the self-congratulatory rush of achieving a second-place finish in the 10,000-metre race set me up for relapse. I had trained for a long time. Furthermore, I had denied myself many rewards to achieve the level of conditioning, required to compete. After such a grueling, hard-fought race, I was over the moon to the extent that I agreed with Little Barry when he whispered in my ear, "You deserve to treat yourself to a celebratory drink." Also, Little Barry wasn't going to let me miss out on the booze fest with the other runners. I should have left the festivities to protect my sobriety, but I wasn't prepared to do that. I had just accomplished an incredible feat, and I thought I could handle anything, even booze. So, I got shit-faced and suffered as I ran the half marathon. I realize now that for an alcoholic, feeling triumphant can be an insidious and dangerous trapdoor that opens after that first drink and drops them into a dark hole of hurt and shame soon after the booze has been pissed away.

I finished the half marathon at the back of the pack. What a loser! I left before the awards were handed out. To stay would have been another reminder of my stupidity because I know I probably would have medaled if I had not gotten pissed.

I returned to the dormitory, took a shower, and then hit the pavement, walking aimlessly for hours, thinking I had thrown my hard-fought abstinence down the toilet for one night of shit-faced bliss. I was wallowing in a sea of guilt and at a crucial juncture in my journey of abstinence. Many alcoholics who fall off the wagon are flooded with despair, shame, and hopelessness. Drowning in guilt and self-recrimination, they give up. They listen to their own version of Little Barry telling them to drink. Thankfully, I didn't take that boozy alternative. When I returned to the dorm, the fog had lifted, and I was feeling much better. I prepared my running gear for the 5,000-metre event and then hit the sack early.

The next day I arrived at the stadium and didn't see the Aussie. Whew! Perhaps this was my race to win. I got the answer when I crossed the finish line in first place! Remarkably, I won the gold medal in a time of eighteen minutes and twenty seconds. Despite the relapse, I felt proud standing on the podium receiving the gold medal and watching the Canadian flag rise to the top of the flagpole. Yes, I had fallen off the wagon, but I had the courage to refocus and return to the "sobriety challenge."

The following day when I flew home, I had plenty of time to think. I was proud that I had placed second in the 10,000-metre race and first in the 5,000-metre race. But the relapse really bothered me. Despite the lingering morass, I vowed to never relapse again. But as every recovering alcoholic knows, keeping that vow is much harder than making it.

CHASING LARRY TALBOT

On July 21, 1981, a ten-year-old girl at Wasaga Beach was abducted in the middle of the night, taken to a nearby vehicle, and sexually assaulted. I was assigned to supervise the investigation. I had a feeling of déjà vu when I noticed the rear door of the house propped open by a rock. I remembered that was Larry Talbot's modus operandi when he used a pail to keep the rear door open at Pat's cottage. Was it a coincidence, or could Talbot be the culprit?[27]

I contacted Sauble Beach to determine if Talbot was still active in their area. Coincidentally, he had been arrested the night before after he was caught prowling near a cottage on Second Avenue. During a brief foot chase, he attempted to discard a pair of leather gloves. He readily admitted stealing lawn chairs and a table and showed the officer where he had stashed the property. When his vehicle was searched, several knives and two pairs of unlined gloves were found in his trunk. He had hidden his wallet under the front seat. Since he was still active, I contacted the Halton Regional Police Service to determine the status of the Pauline Ivy Dudley homicide.

PAULINE IVY DUDLEY

I learned of the homicide of Pauline Ivy Dudley, on Sept. 15, 1973, when an Oakville PD (Now Halton Regional Police) contacted me because Talbot was the prime suspect. (The officer called because he wanted information on our cottage break-in.) Pauline was last seen on August 19, 1973, after leaving her mother's residence on Lakeshore Blvd. in Oakville. She was travelling to her residence in the Milton area. On August 28, her body was discovered in a farmer's field at the corner of Lower Baseline Road and Highway 25. Talbot became a person of interest after an officer checked an unoccupied vehicle on August 10 in Henderson Park north of Oakville. It was approximately a mile from the location where Dudley's body was discovered two weeks later. The officer noted the licence plate and gave the information to the detectives investigating the homicide. The vehicle was registered to Talbot, who was living in Burlington. On Sept. 5, the detectives searched Talbot's vehicle. They discovered a small splotch of blood on the driver's headrest and a clump of hair on the rear floor. (A subsequent forensic analysis determined the hair was

---

27   Specimens obtained from the victim were forwarded to the Centre of Forensic Sciences in Toronto, and a subsequent analysis eliminated Talbot as the perpetrator. The assault remains a cold case.

similar to Dudley's but in the pre-DNA era, that was the best they could do.) When the trunk was searched, they discovered a rape kit, which included an artificial penis, a jar of Vaseline, a tube of desensitizing cream, surgical gloves, hockey laces, leather gloves, a hunting knife, surgical tape, and a roll of wire.

I contacted Halton Regional Police and was advised that Talbot was still the prime suspect in the Dudley homicide. However, there was insufficient evidence to indict him. Nevertheless, I was interested in reviewing the reports. One paragraph caught my attention (emphasis added): "An extensive investigation was conducted on him [Talbot] including a polygraph and forensic work etc., but with negative results (including surveillance.) *We still strongly believe he is the man responsible.*" A plethora of incriminating evidence linked Talbot to the Dudley homicide. He lived in Burlington, fifteen minutes from the crime scene. He admitted to being in the park, a splotch of blood was found on the driver's headrest, a clump of hair similar to Dudley's was recovered from his vehicle, and a rape kit was found in his trunk. He also had a history of violence, including the break-in at Pat's cottage. After reviewing the reports, I was left with a frightening thought: were there other victims?

CHRISTINE PRINCE AND DELIA ADRIANO

Christine Prince was last seen in Toronto riding on a St. Clair streetcar on June 23, 1982, at about 1:30 a.m. Her body was discovered later that morning in the Rouge River near Sewell's Road and Finch Avenue East in Scarborough. It was approximately 30 km from the location where she was abducted. There was evidence of sexual assault. Coincidentally, Talbot resided in Scarborough, and I learned from a credit card contact that he was at Tramps, a bar in Toronto, on the night Prince was abducted.

On Sunday, September 26, 1982, Delia Adriano, and her boyfriend attended a soccer match. Following the game, he dropped her off at her residence in Oakville. Her naked body was discovered on November 6, 1982, in a wooded area, near the second line and Side Road 3 in Milton approximately 30 km from her residence. The homicides of Pauline Dudley, Christine Prince, and Delia Adriano were strikingly similar. They were young females, had been sexually assaulted, were discovered in wilderness areas, their bodies hadn't been concealed, and the crimes occurred after dark.

On February 3, 1983, I travelled to Toronto to determine the distance between the Prince crime scene and Talbot's residence and the distance between Adriano and Talbot's places of work. I also met with Les Church, who had worked with Talbot at Industrial Plumbing* from 1959–1960.

The distance from Talbot's residence to the bridge on Sewell's road where Christine's body was discovered was eight kilometres. It took me eight minutes and fifty-one seconds to drive there. The distance from Talbot's workplace to Wear Check, where Delia worked, was only two kilometres. This was interesting, but was it merely a coincidence?

Les Church had taken over the Industrial Plumbing territory previously covered by Talbot in January 1960. Les had been a character witness when Talbot was convicted for breaking into Pat's cottage. I explained that Talbot was a person of interest in a homicide. Fortunately, he was very cooperative. He told me Talbot was a loner. When Talbot was incarcerated at the Mimico Correctional Facility, Church was the only person to visit him. (He was serving six months for possessing burglary tools.) He also recalled Talbot confessing that "something came over him" and he, wasn't "in control of himself" when he committed crimes. He told Les he saw a psychiatrist at the Clarke Institute, but "the guy didn't do anything for him."

I was interested in the territory that Church covered, and he showed me the locations on a map, including Clinton. I asked who he visited in Clinton. "

The Clinton Air Force Base," he replied. Immediately I recalled the Lynne Harper homicide. She was murdered on June 9, 1959, when the Clinton Air Force Base was Talbot's customer.

PROJECT TREE

On February 4, 1983, I briefed D/Sgt. Browning on my interview with Les Church. I suggested that the OPP may have arrested the wrong person for the Lynne Harper homicide. He instructed me not to mention the Harper homicide in the report requesting surveillance. He didn't elaborate, but I figured advancing the Harper-Talbot hypothesis was likely to raise a few eyebrows because it meant Harold Graham, the lead investigator, who had gone on to become the OPP commissioner, may have arrested the wrong person. I understood why Browning wasn't comfortable signing off on a report that essentially critiqued Graham's investigation, but there was circumstantial evidence implicating Talbot, and I reasoned that at the very least he should have been questioned.

When I left the office, I called Les Church. He reiterated what he said in the initial interview. However, this time I recorded the conversation.[28] He related that Talbot would likely visit the Air Force Base four to six times a year. After speaking to Church, I called Bill Elliott*, who also worked with Talbot. I wondered if he remembered the vehicle Talbot drove in 1959. He recalled that Talbot drove a baby-blue two-door 1957 Chevrolet. (Steven Truscott was questioned on June 10 and told an officer that Lynne got into a "late-model Chevrolet with lots of chrome.") I requested he keep our conversation to himself. I completed my report, heeding Browning's instructions to keep Lynne Harper out of the report, even though, I thought that the responsible thing to do was to include her.

I sent the report to GHQ on March 15 and hoped it would persuade the brass to approve surveillance. I received the answer when Project Tree was launched March 31, 1983. The OPP intelligence "spin team" was assigned to monitor Talbot's movements. I wondered if Talbot would act out.

While I wasn't privy to the ongoing surveillance, a buddy on the spin team told me they followed him to a strip joint in Buffalo, watched him steal hubcaps from a vehicle, and drive through a lover's lane in the middle of the night. They also surreptitiously gained entry to his vehicle and discovered a rape kit in the trunk. I thought it was just a matter of time before they collar him.

Unfortunately, disaster struck on May 4 when Talbot was stopped on Highway 11 near Orillia for speeding. The officer conducted a Canadian Police Information Centre (CPIC) request on Talbot, and Talbot overheard the dispatcher name him as the prime suspect in the Pauline Dudley homicide. (Prior to the implementation of Project Tree, I entered Talbot's licence plate number on CPIC with the expectation that if Talbot's unattended vehicle was checked, it would be a red flag for an officer to check the area for him.) On May 18, I was talking to my buddy from headquarters who advised me that the project was being scaled down, and I was being blamed for leaving Talbot on the CPIC system. A sad finale indeed! I worried that the wolf in sheep's clothing was now free to roam unfettered!

---

28 My rationale for recording the conversation included the notion that if the Lynne Harper case was reopened, and I died, the conversations would be available for the investigation. This was prophetic. A transcript of the tapes was given to Steven Truscott's lawyer at his 2007 appeal. Ironically, I experienced two near-death experiences before that: a battle with prostate cancer in 1996 and a near drowning in 1997 in Cuba (see chapter eight).

SELF-REFLECTION

I was obsessed with Talbot, believing he could be a serial killer. I spoke about him incessantly with family, friends, and police personnel. I spent many sleepless nights ruminating about him. I also had a terrifying nightmare when Talbot sprang from a laundry basket screaming and pointing a gun at me. Furthermore, I experienced bouts of anxiety, frustration, and anger. If not for running, I probably would have returned to booze to self-medicate. Little Barry took every opportunity to urge me to drink. He pestered me with statements like "This is bull-shit. Anyone would drink under these circumstances" or "Talbot is out there, victimizing young women, and there's nothing you can do about it. So, you might as well have a drink, just one drink." I knew that a couple of drinks might numb my feelings, but the relief would be short-lived. So, I held fast to my commitment not to drink and continued to run daily. Running helped, but I was experiencing crushing chest pains. Pat insisted I see our doctor. He thought my symptoms were stress related and prescribed Lorazepam to relieve my anxiety. Going forward, the combination of running and medication helped somewhat, but I still experienced occasional discomfort. I continued ruminating about Talbot, wondering, if I would have another opportunity to take a run at him.

ROBBERY WITH VIOLENCE—MIDLAND DETACHMENT

On Saturday, July 23, 1983, I was enjoying an early morning run when my pager went off, and I was advised that an elderly man living near Midland had been attacked and robbed. The victim had been walking along the roadway in Tay Township at approximately 8:00 p.m. on July 22 when he was attacked and left in a ditch. A passerby found the victim, and he was transported to a hospital in Toronto. I interviewed him, and even though his injuries were serious, he managed to tell me there was $500 in his wallet. He also remembered walking by a red pickup truck just before being struck on the head, but he couldn't describe the assailant. When I was leaving, I wished him well and wondered if anyone would visit him.

My partner and I canvassed the area where the attack occurred, with no luck. However, we learned the victim was a loner and known as "the hermit." It was frustrating rapping on doors and coming up empty—until a woman saw an OPP media release and knew a teenager who owned a red pickup truck. His name was William Jeffrey*, and he lived approximately two kilometres west of the crime scene. A query on CPIC revealed a William Jeffrey from Tay Township had a criminal record for theft and assault.

I called Jeffrey and told him I was investigating a robbery in the vicinity where he lived. (I conned him into thinking I just wanted to know if he had witnessed anything.) He agreed to meet the next day. Prior to the interview, I hid a briefcase containing a tape recorder in the room. If we arrested him, the recording could be introduced at trial.

My partner and I began asking Jeffrey softball questions about his employment and relationships. When he appeared relaxed, we hit him with the hardballs. He readily admitted to knowing the victim but vehemently denied attacking him. He related that on the evening of the robbery, he was playing pool at the Harbor Light Hotel* with his buddy Doug Cash*. He said he left the hotel at approximately 8:30 p.m. If true, he appeared to have an ironclad alibi.

When the interview was finished, I asked if he would submit to a polygraph examination. (The results cannot be introduced at trial, but it could implicate or exonerate him as a person of interest.) He politely declined, and I wondered why.

The following day, I called Cash, and he agreed to meet with us. While I was watching for him, a classic 1957 Chevrolet rolled into the parking lot, Jeffrey was in the front seat. *Oh shit,* I thought, *they colluded*. But I reasoned that if they had, the "sameness" of their respective stories would assist in the investigation.

As with Jeffrey, I began the interview by asking him softball questions. I learned that he and Jeffrey were childhood pals, so it was even more conceivable he would lie for his buddy. So, I cut to the chase and asked him about playing pool with Jeffrey on the evening of the robbery. Surprisingly, he said they finished playing at around 7:00 p.m., which didn't coincide with Jeffrey's story. So, what were they doing between 7:00 and 8:30 p.m., and why had Jeffrey lied?

I updated D/Sgt. Browning on our progress and advised him that I'd be preoccupied transcribing the recordings. At the outset I didn't realize how arduous a task lay ahead—listening to a snippet, pausing the recorder, noting the comments, and repeating the process. It didn't take long before I was stressed to the max! Enter Insp. Dave Almond, who asked how long before the transcribing was complete! "Fuck it, I'm going home!" I exclaimed as I grabbed my briefcase. "I'm going on holidays." With that, I stormed out of the office.

THE HOLIDAY FROM HELL

Usually, I enjoyed the beauty and solitude of our pristine paradise on Bucktooth Island. However, my blow up haunted me from the moment I stepped foot there. Throughout our vacation, I was preoccupied with futile attempts to block the ruminations about my meltdown and the consequences when I returned to work. I was overwhelmed with feelings of anxiety and guilt. I had screwed up big time! For the first time in my life, I started to question who Barry Ruhl was and my inexplicable reaction to a reasonable question: "Fuck it, I'm going home!" Really? What was I thinking? I realized I wasn't.

SELF-REFLECTION

Much later in my life, I understood some narcissistic features of my personality that were problematic. At their core, narcissistic personalities harbor well-entrenched and suppressed feelings of inferiority, incompetence, and helplessness accompanied by profound feelings of shame and fear. They are ashamed of who they are and afraid they will be "found out," Essentially, the shame is learned during their childhood years and, therefore, is for the most part, inaccessible to them. Also, these thoughts and feelings are incomprehensible and intolerable. So, during their developmental years, they construct a "public" narcissistic personality, which serves to help them suppress and deny the unacceptable parts of themselves. This public personality presents socially as overconfidence and entitlement to special treatment. They bolster their fragile self-esteem and suppress their feelings by seeking the praise and admiration of others, especially people they see as special or powerful, like supervisors, which brings me back to my blow up.

With the benefit of time, experience, and self-analysis, I have some understanding of my narcissistic reaction in that situation. I was hoping to shine like the bright star that I thought (i.e., hoped) I was. Furthermore, I was seeking the praise and admiration of my supervisors, to which I thought I was entitled. I had taken on too much and was about to prove the very thing I was terrified of. So, when the inspector asked how much longer it would take to transcribe the tapes, I was flooded with fear and shame that was so profound and all-encompassing that it overwhelmed my good judgment, causing me to want to escape, no matter the cost. Rather than basking in glory, I was revealing the incompetence and shame that washes over a narcissist when presented with evidence that he or she is like everyone else: nothing special. I hated to be perceived as just one of the crowd. Why else would I bust my ass to win a 10,000-metre race? However, in this situation, I saw myself as a failure and, worse yet, I made an ass of myself, proving that I was unworthy of the very admiration I craved. When Insp. Almond asked how long the transcription would take, my self-esteem exploded like a hand grenade, leaving everyone around me shell-shocked and asking, "What the hell has gotten into him?" That was the question I was going to face when I returned, which would be another attack on my narcissism.

NARCISSISM AND ALCOHOLISM

As you might imagine, suppressing and denying one's core shame can be intense, leaving a person feeling stressed. This typically manifests itself in profound and pervasive physiological and psychological tension.[29] Because alcohol is a depressant with sedative effects, one or two drinks results in a reduction of physiological tension (i.e., relaxation) and an increased sense of well-being. On the downside, the drinker also experiences disinhibition, which can lead to increased alcohol consumption. The disciplined drinker possesses the ability and self-awareness to regulate his or her drinking according to the social context. However, the alcoholic with a robust narcissistic personality is more likely to drink inappropriately and excessively. Although it may seem contradictory, narcissists believe they are always in control.

Without alcohol, my presentation of self was always edgy, especially socializing with folks I didn't know. *What will they think of me? Will I be accepted? Will I say something embarrassing?* Consequently, if I didn't drink beforehand, my suppressed inadequacies emerged, urging me to fade into the woodwork like a wallflower. This behaviour was most prevalent when I attended functions where prominent individuals were present. The more prominent and important a person was, the more my feelings of inferiority prompted me to disappear. But if I was drinking, party! My inhibitions went out the window, and I schmoozed with everyone.

Alcohol became a crutch during my teen years. After several drinks, my underlying feelings of inadequacy were replaced with an enhanced sense of well-being. The secret to turning the corner on my narcissistic alcoholism was learning to accept myself as I am. I

---

29   Psychological tension is a term I use to cover all emotional problems. This includes anxiety and panic in all its guises. It covers depression and painful low moods and stresses brought about by relationships and family worries. Anger and frustration are also forms of psychological tension, as is the grating sense of dissatisfaction and unhappiness many of us feel (https://emotionalskills.uk/blog/what-is-psychological-tension).

didn't change (i.e., stop drinking) until I realized and accepted that I was the same person, drunk or sober. I also learned I was much more likeable when I was sober. Once I overcame my shyness and shame, I learned to be more comfortable in social situations. I also learned that I had something to say, but more importantly, I learned that listening to others was a great way to get to know people. Over time, I learned to accept myself and my shortcomings rather than allow them to trigger my shame. Nevertheless, I still need to remind myself constantly that I don't need to be the star. However, this self-analysis amounts to nothing the minute I take a drink.

THE ARBITRARY HAND OF THE OPP

When my holiday from hell ended, I reluctantly returned to work. As I drove home, I imagined the chilly reception awaiting me. So, I wasn't surprised when D/Sgt. Browning asked if I'd had a nice holiday, which seemed like an obvious prelude to a dressing down. He said that he and Inspector Almond were concerned about my inappropriate behavior. I said the meltdown was caused by stress while transcribing the tapes. I apologized for my outlandish behavior, but he didn't respond. (In this situation, silence wasn't golden!) Why was he taking so long? Was I going to be blindsided? Finally, he accepted my apology. It felt like a heavy weight had been lifted from me. Unfortunately, the Midland investigation had been closed because there wasn't sufficient evidence to indict Jeffrey. So, in the end, transcribing the tapes had been all for naught. Jeffrey beat the system, and I had potentially jeopardized my career with the meltdown. However, I continued enthusiastically as the CIS coordinator, relieved that D/Sgt. Browning and I were working together as a team. Unfortunately, our harmonious relationship was the calm before the storm.

On October 17, 1983, D/Sgt. Browning advised me that Supt. Burkett wanted a review of my work performance. I was gobsmacked. He explained that GHQ wasn't happy with the Talbot report, noting there were comments in the narrative that weren't factual. I was stunned. As far as I was concerned, that was bullshit! What the hell was going on? I asked Browning if he knew what was in the report that wasn't factual. He said he didn't know, simply noting that there had been a complaint. This was unbelievable! I had been accused of penning false information and investigated for an accusation that was patently false. It was mind-boggling. Ironically, an individual accused of committing a crime had to be advised of the details of the offence, whereas I, a member of the OPP, wasn't afforded that same right. He also mentioned that a CIB inspector complained about my performance at a homicide investigation. He was referring to the murder of a woman in the Bradford detachment area. I was involved in the investigation for two days. However, I was a member of the OPP running team, scheduled to compete in the Detroit Police Games, so I arranged for Cpl. John Allan of the Bradford detachment to assist the CIB inspector. I had called Supt. Burkett and advised him of the arrangement, and he didn't object.

I was angry, hurt, and confused. Why did the superintendent require a review? D/Sgt. Browning was satisfied with my performance and asserted in my Aug. 1981 to Sept. 1982 annual performance evaluation that my performance was "Excellent" and noted I was instrumental in bringing several major crimes to successful conclusion. He also referenced a letter of commendation from Commissioner H. H. Graham for my work on Project SCAM in Bracebridge. The evaluation was forwarded to Supt. Burkett, who added: "I concur with the contents of this report. I'm aware of this member's position and it is gratifying to see that he is performing so well." You can imagine my confusion when I received my Sept. 1982 to Sept. 1983 performance evaluation dated twenty-five days before I was gobsmacked by the phony accusation. In that evaluation, D/Sgt. Browning commented that my "devotion to duty cannot be questioned." However, he added that my efforts as the CIS crime coordinator had been misdirected. Furthermore, he complained that I didn't conduct a thorough crime scene search at the Midland robbery, as follows (emphasis added):

It should be noted that these comments don't reflect a sudden change in Corporal Ruhl's performance. These comments are made because the writer [referring to himself in the third person] *in the past short period of time* became aware of the shortcomings. The writer has not had time to initiate meaningful corrective action and these comments are made for the purpose of spelling out the problems so a starting point can be determined to correct them. I have no doubt that given the proper direction, Cpl. Ruhl will make every effort and is fully capable of performing his duties properly.

The evaluation was forwarded to Supt. Burkett, who added, "I concur with the comments and it's anticipated that Corporal Ruhl will receive the proper direction and make every effort to perform his duties properly. He must also realize that we all have to be prepared to accept constructive criticism from our supervisors for the betterment of the Force."

MOVING ON

But that wasn't going to happen. D/Sgt. Browning advised me that I was being transferred to the Barrie detachment. I was dumbfounded and disoriented. I advised him I needed time off and then quickly left the office. I couldn't make sense of anything, least of all the questionable allegations regarding the Talbot report.

When I arrived home, Pat was in the kitchen. She asked why I was home early. I told her I was being transferred to Barrie. Pat stared at me momentarily and then said she was sorry. I hunkered down in the house, depressed and grieving the loss of my dream job. I also reminisced about my contributions, including implementation of the CIS squad, coordinating undercover projects, and supervising major investigations. Now, for very tenuous reasons, I was being banished! I was depressed, angry, and I had no appetite. I languished in the living room with the drapes drawn listening to our grandfather clock tick. Meanwhile, Little Barry was coaxing me to have a drink. But I resisted, recalling the shit-storms that had accompanied my booze binges.

Pat became increasingly concerned that I might kill myself. She called a doctor friend who didn't think I would. However, I did think about shooting myself with my service revolver. But juxtaposed with suicidal ideation was my love for Pat and Jeffrey. I realized killing myself was a selfish and permanent solution to a temporary problem that would haunt them for a lifetime.

After mulling over my dilemma, I decided to meet Supt. Burkett and attempt to save my job. Once I had that goal in mind, my mood and attitude changed. I requested a meeting with him for the following morning. Then I focused all my energy on a defense. I was going to remind Supt. Burkett that I had called him prior to attending the Detroit Police Games, and he hadn't objected to me going. I also wanted to confirm that there weren't any fabrications in the Talbot report. I thought I was prepared for the meeting, but I wondered if he would listen.

On October 20, 1983, I arrived at district headquarters. I recalled our initial meeting when he welcomed me with open arms. When I entered the building, I noticed several officers gawking at me. Did they know about my fall from grace?

I trudged up the stairs to his office and knocked timidly on his door. I was greeted with a terse "Enter!" He asked what I had to say. I remained standing and reminded him that I had called regarding my attendance at the Detroit Police Games and said Cpl. Allan from the Bradford detachment would assist in my stead. I also insisted that everything in the Larry Talbot report was factually correct. Remarkably, he didn't address those issues. Instead, he said I had lost credibility with the CIB, and Dep. Comm. Bill Lidstone wanted me removed from the unit. He said the force had spent thousands of dollars on Project Tree, but Larry Talbot had not been apprehended. End of discussion!

Before leaving, I asked him to arrange a meeting with Dr. John Sawatzy, the OPP psychologist. This debacle was extremely stressful, and I was also obsessing about Larry Talbot and the possibility that he was still victimizing women.

On the way home, I thought about the shit-storm. On October 17, D/Sgt. Browning informed me there were fabrications in the Talbot report, but I was never informed of the context and never questioned. My best guess was there probably wasn't an investigation. I couldn't help but wonder if my insistence on reopening the Lynne Harper homicide was the rationale for dumping me. In retrospect, questioning a homicide investigated by Harold Graham, who served as commissioner of the OPP from 1973 to 1981, was a game changer!

MEETING DR. JOHN SAWATZKY

On November 5, 1984, I met Dr. John Sawatzky at general headquarters. "Dr. John," as he was affectionately called, remembered speaking with me during the corporal promotional competition and recalled my "executive potential." Although his recollection made me feel better, I was hoping he could help me alleviate the obsessive thoughts that my nemesis might be preying on women. He opined that my thoughts, feelings, and behaviours were self-defeating. He suggested I "burn the files" and get on with my life. I thanked Dr. John for seeing me and then left. It didn't make any sense to discard the files, so I stored them in a secure place and continued to monitor Talbot's movements, as documented in *A Viable Suspect*.

CHAPTER 7

BARRIE DETACHMENT

ON THE ROAD AGAIN

REGARDLESS OF HOW UNFAIR AND arbitrary, the die was cast, and I was back in uniform.[30] Although I was disappointed, I was somewhat excited to test my mettle in an entirely different role. However, I decided to enter the Donwood Institute in Toronto before beginning at Barrie. Even though I quit drinking in 1973, I was devastated, angry, and depressed. After the questionable transfer, it seemed like nothing really mattered when I fell off the proverbial wagon.

The relapse occurred when Pat was working, and Jeffrey was in school. I was engaged in what the addiction literature refers to as "stinky thinking." I felt like I would never be a member of CIB. I felt like I was damaged goods. I felt worthless, and in that mindset, I was vulnerable to Little Barry. So, instead of calling Alcoholics Anonymous (AA) or anyone else who could help, I resorted to my "friend," the bottle.

When Pat returned from work, she found me passed out in the living room and several bottles of liquor on the kitchen counter, which she found incomprehensible. Apparently, I had been switching from one bottle to another. Clearly, I didn't care about myself, my job, or, apparently, my family. At that point, although I would have denied it, I was attempting "suicide by alcohol."

---

30 The expression of "back in the bag" or "back to uniform" is quite common in policing circles. I know it sounds like being in uniform is a demotion, but it is not. I was still a sergeant (the corporal rank had been phased out by then); I was just now working in uniform. Even so, returning to uniform felt like a demotion. I had worked my ass off to get into the CIB, and now I was "going back." Nevertheless, many police officers do not want to work in the CIB. They like the uniform, and to them it is a symbol of their work and their professionalism.

SELF-REFLECTION

I mentioned earlier that prior to meeting Supt. Burkett, I had considered but rejected the idea of suicide. Now I wonder if binging straight liquor was an attempt to kill myself. I don't know if I was subconsciously motivated to drink myself to death, but it sure looked that way. Now that I have left that dark place and written this book, I can wholeheartedly say I'm glad I didn't perish. So many wonderful things have happened in my life since that crisis. Nevertheless, during that dreadful time, in the black hole of despair, I felt nothing but anguish. And it wasn't helpful when I woke up and Jeffrey kissed me goodnight, saying, "Oh, Daddy, you stink!" Reality check! I knew I had screwed up big time in the eyes of my son. I was still too drunk to plan any remedial action, but when I sobered up, I realized I needed help!

TO GO OR NOT TO GO, THAT IS THE QUESTION

I contacted the Donwood Institute in Toronto because it had an excellent reputation in the addiction field. I was added to the waiting list, but I wondered if I had made the right decision. I was experiencing a free-floating anxiety about the program. Stinky thinking enveloped my psyche. What if it wasn't all it was cracked up to be? (Nowadays, I know that the Donwood Institute is renowned as one of the premium treatment facilities in Canada. Over 15,000 clients have received treatment there since 1967, and the recovery rate is an impressive 65 percent.)

I was also intrigued that the Donwood Institute emphasized an egalitarian approach to treatment. Essentially, it didn't matter if clients were wealthy or poor, famous or obscure; the Donwood Institute treated everyone. Finally, and fortunately, it qualified as a public hospital, which meant their fees were covered by the Ontario Hospital Insurance Plan. Ultimately, I decided that my need for treatment far outweighed my fear of treatment. Little Barry was constantly bugging me to drink, and without help, it was only a matter of time before I relapsed.

THE DONWOOD EXPERIENCE

On the day I was to go, I awoke feeling anxious and ruminating about my decision. My uneasiness remained as I drove to Toronto. Surprisingly, when I arrived and walked toward the entrance, I noticed empty mini bottles of liquor blanketing the ground. I thought perhaps the new arrivals had a last hoist before entering the program.

I anxiously opened the ornate door. Thankfully, I was greeted by a smiling receptionist, who shook my hand. Her friendly disposition and caring manner reinforced the notion that this was where I belonged. Following registration, a counsellor escorted me to the auditorium, where the other new arrivals were assembling. As we waited for Executive Director Dr. David Korn to welcome us, silence underscored the palpable fear of the unknown.

I glanced around and noticed several patients wearing towels around their necks. I learned they were experiencing severe withdrawal symptoms, and some had completed a medical monitored detox, because they had been experiencing delirium tremens (DTs)[31] They were treated in a unit known affectionately and ironically as "Happy Valley." I was heartened when I spotted a nurse wrapping a towel around the neck of a middle-aged man nearby.

When she left, we introduced ourselves. His name was Marcel, and he had been the proprietor of an interior decorating business until it went south because of his drinking. I couldn't help thinking that the same thing could happen to me. I could lose Pat, Jeffrey, my career, everything. I was determined to not let that happen.

WORKING THE PROGRAM

The program included exercise classes, group therapy, life skills, information about drugs and alcohol, nutritional education, relapse prevention, stress management, and spiritual health. The members of my therapy group included a fireman, an executive manager, a housewife, a laborer, a retired politician, an interior decorator, and a bank executive.

During the first session as we waited for the counsellor, nobody spoke. The silence was anxiety provoking. When the counsellor arrived, she introduced herself and explained the group dynamics. Essentially, the program allowed us to share our thoughts and feelings. She also said that "Whatever's said in the room, stays in the room! And if someone didn't want to share, say 'pass.'" The friendly demeanor, and guidance, was a welcome relief.

The program was exhausting but constructive and positive. It was heart wrenching listening to the plight of others but comforting to have a safe place to share my fears

---

31 Delirium tremens is a severe form of alcohol withdrawal. It involves sudden and severe mental or nervous system changes (https://medlineplus.gov/ency/article/000766.htm).

and resentments. I revisited my banishment from the Crime Until incessantly. I couldn't understand why the CIB had lost confidence in me. My thoughts were like a gyroscope, spinning out of control. Larry Talbot's violation of Pat's cottage that night. The likelihood that he was a serial killer. The Lynne Harper homicide investigated by Harold Graham, retired OPP commissioner. My report and the allegation that it was not factual, and the inference that I was a thorn in the side of the OPP because I believed Steven Truscott had been wrongfully convicted. I felt like I was being screwed by the organization that I had considered my family for nineteen years.

The counsellor thought I was stuck in a quagmire and essentially going in circles. She suggested I see the resident psychiatrist. I met with him and shared my incessant ruminations about Larry Talbot, the OPP's unfair treatment of me, and my belief that Truscott was wrongfully accused. The psychiatrist remained silent throughout. When I finished, he simply said, "Steven Truscott knows if he's culpable, and that's what really matters." That was the extent of the session! I expected he could help with the recurring issues, but instead he proffered a simplistic observation. Unbelievable. However, I think the group dynamics helped somewhat.

As the weeks progressed, we became close. Essentially clinging to a raft, afloat in troubled waters, we cried, hugged, and even laughed. And we survived. When I left the Donwood, I had a much better understanding of myself without the need to seek solace in a bottle.

ONE DAY AT A TIME

In, *The Big Book of Alcoholics Anonymous*, Bill Wilson, the founder of AA, says, "On a day-at-a-time basis, I am confident I can stay away from a drink for one day. So, I set out with confidence. At the end of the day, I have the reward of achievement. Achievement feels good and that makes me want more!" Essentially, he understood the therapeutic value of manageable increments, which answers the question, "How do you eat an elephant?" Answer: one mouthful at a time. I adopted Wilson's principle as my mantra.

Unfortunately, two members of the group relapsed. On a beautiful summer afternoon, I had just finished a run and was feeling fantastic. Then my phone rang. It was Marcel, and he was drunk. My heart sank. He was calling from Eugene's house. Eugene was the banker in the group, and he had reached out to Marcel because he had a fight with his brother. But calling Marcel was a mistake. Marcel went to Eugene's house with a bottle of vodka, which they promptly polished off! Marcel's call was unsettling. I suggested he contact the Donwood to get help. He wasn't listening and was babbling incoherently, so I hung up.

A week later, he called again, but it was more ominous. He was very drunk, but this time he was threatening to kill himself! I attempted to discover his whereabouts, but he hung up. Frantic, I called the Donwood and suggested they contact the police. After the call, I was fraught with worry. A few days later, a counsellor called and said that Marcel had been located but didn't elaborate. I remember listening to the plight of Marcel and Eugene during group sessions and thinking both were struggling with issues. Unfortunately, the Donwood couldn't help them sustain sobriety. Regrettably, I lost contact with them both, and I can only hope they were survivors.

SELF-REFLECTION

I thought about my relapses, especially the last one that took me to the edge of suicide. I felt worthless, helpless, and hopeless. It was a stark contrast to the unconquerable high I felt after winning the race in Texas. It's the exquisite highs and the abject lows that cause addicts to relapse. Even though I didn't realize it, when I was kicked out of the Crime Unit, booze was still my coping strategy of last resort. I had been coasting in a fool's paradise, thinking I had mastered the "art" of abstinence. I call it a fool's paradise because I was foolish to think that without "working the program," I would never relapse. Essentially, I needed to accept the reality that I was rendered powerless when I drank and accept that alcohol affected my reasoning and control. And I don't mean just in my head. I had to accept my inability to control alcohol physically, socially, emotionally, and spiritually. The paradox of treatment is to learn how to be secure while accepting one's vulnerabilities.

Another vital component is learning about the process of relapsing. As a sober, untreated alcoholic, I didn't understand that my potential to relapse could sneak up and bite me. That is, I always thought that a relapse would start with my first drink. No! Now I realize that my last relapse began when I became angry and frustrated transcribing those tapes. The progression intensified when I had the meltdown and later when I learned that my report on Talbot was called into question. Consequently, when I was told I had been kicked out of the Crime Unit, my relapse was well underway. Essentially, I was physically, emotionally, socially, and spiritually empty, defenseless. I didn't have any resources remaining to fight off Little Barry. Now, I'm more aware of what my emotions are telling me. Furthermore, I have social supports ready to help me. I'm also more spiritually centered, and have a plan with specific steps, should Little Barry try to trap me. Deciding to go for treatment is one of the most important decisions I made.

FEELING THE PRIDE

On the eve of reporting for duty, I laid awake, feeling distressed and ruminating about the unwelcome transfer and the reception I'd receive. Would I be accepted? Was I capable of supervising a platoon? Would I enjoy shift work? Most importantly, did I want to remain on the force?

The next morning as I put on my uniform, my anxiety spiked, and I was flooded by thoughts and emotions associated with the traumatic events that I had encountered as a street cop. However, when I finished putting on "the blue," I swelled with the same sense of pride that I felt when I joined the OPP. Nevertheless, it was overshadowed, or at least diminished, by a feeling that I was damaged goods and needed to prove myself once again.

Much to my relief, I was greeted with a handshake from the first officer I met. As the morning progressed, I gradually relaxed. It seemed my platoon was eager to help me adjust. It wasn't long before they nicknamed me "Dad," a name I considered an expression of affection and acceptance. The officers assigned to general law enforcement are, to a large extent, the backbone of the organization. They are exposed to every type of occurrence, from the trivial to the tragic, and I can state unequivocally that the officers I had the privilege of supervising were second to none.

THE SPIKE BELT DEBACLE

The vision that most people have of policing is from television and the movies. Typically, TV cops are chasing bandits ad infinitum. However, to a large extent, policing is mundane, with few hair-raising episodes. Nevertheless, "Dad" still enjoyed "cruising," and on occasion I partnered with a platoon member. To a large extent, the patrols were not nearly exciting as TV shows. However, during one otherwise quiet midnight shift, that wasn't the case.

I was patrolling with a recruit when the comm. centre advised that a van had taken a run at an undercover cop in Toronto and was being pursued by units from Toronto, York Regional Police, and the OPP. The van was travelling northbound on Highway 400 at speeds nearing 160 kph! Coincidentally, the detachment had recently acquired a spike belt. However, neither the recruit, nor I were trained in its use. But what could possibly go wrong if we deployed it?

We waited at the intersection of Highways 400 and 97. It wasn't long before I heard the wailing sirens approaching. I instructed the recruit to set up in the southbound lanes and listen for my instructions. When it was showtime, I yelled, "Let it go!" As expected, the belt flew into the northbound lanes, but it missed the van and nailed an OPP cruiser!

I cringed when I heard the officer advise the comm. centre that he was out of commission. *Oh shit! I'm going to hear about that!*

Nevertheless, there was no time for mea culpas. The parade of cruisers continued northbound on Hwy 400 until the van made a U-turn near Orillia and headed southbound. We hid behind an abutment adjacent to the Hwy 400 extension, and when the van approached, this time the toss was on the money, and the front tires began to deflate. Nevertheless, the crippled vehicle limped about a kilometre before stopping, surrounded by cruisers. The bandit surrendered, which was a wise move considering the plethora of weapons trained on him. So, apart from the tire damage to the OPP cruiser, no one was injured, and we took a bad guy off the street. And yes, we received spike belt training.

TRAPPED IN A SILO

One request, causes officers to head for the exits: "Who wants to ride the pony?" This is a euphemism for desk duty—receiving calls from the public. Although it may sound simple, it's very challenging because the officer must decide if a call is an emergency while also watching for incoming calls on the other lines. Riding the pony was far from appealing for the platoon, so I became the designated desk-duty officer. It was a wise decision because I maintained a full complement of officers on the road.

As I cut my teeth for the first couple of weeks, the calls were mundane. But that was about to change!

"OPP Barrie, Sergeant Ruhl," I said.

"Help!" the caller screamed. "My grandson and his friend are trapped in a silo!" I was momentarily disoriented but managed to assure the caller that I was sending help. Unfortunately, I knew if they weren't extricated quickly, they would suffocate. A profound feeling of helplessness washed over me.

The comm. centre dispatched an ambulance. However, regrettably, the eight-year-old boys died. My heart ached for their families. I thought about my son and how devastating it would be to hear he had died under such terrible circumstances. During the remainder of the shift, I thought about the grandfather's frantic call, and his panicked pleading reverberated within me. I imagined the boys had been doing what I did as a kid: playing with chums, oblivious to the dangers of the world, and now they were dead.

Although that call was tragic, there were other alarming calls. For example, a caller was at a party and reported a double murder had just occurred. Whenever, I rode the pony, I'd stare at the telephone and wonder what the next call would entail.

A CALLER'S CONFESSION

I received a call from a man who complained about a drunk refusing to leave his residence. Unalarmed, I advised him I'd dispatch an officer as soon as possible. That response was unacceptable, and he ranted about the "the piss-poor service" and then hung up. His belligerent manner concerned me, and I was about to dispatch two officers. But before I did, he called back. "Well, you guys didn't show, so I shot the guy," he said. For a moment, I was stunned. But when I made sense of the utterance, I instructed him to unload the weapon, place it in the driveway, and sit on the porch with his hands in plain view. I rushed to the scene with backup units and the nagging feeling I might be in trouble for not dispatching officers following the initial call.

We cautiously entered the driveway, and I spotted the shooter sitting on the porch. I also noticed a rifle with an open breech lying in the driveway. I approached the shooter, who was remarkably calm, compliant, and responsive. When I asked him the whereabouts of the victim, he said he was in the marsh behind the house.

I requested the canine unit because the dog would likely find the victim quicker than us. When "Golden" and the handler arrived, I brought him up to speed, and we headed into the marsh. Suddenly, Golden, began barking and took off running. When we caught up, I spotted the victim lying beside a stream. He was bleeding from a leg wound but able to walk with our assistance. The investigation revealed the boozing buddies had been drinking, and the shooter had asked his buddy to leave. He refused, resulting in the shooter's initial call. Instead of waiting for the police, the shooter took matters into his own hands. When the visitor refused to leave, the shooter pointed a rifle at him, and the "guest" grabbed the barrel, causing the rifle to discharge. Consequently, I charged the owner with weapon-related offences. He pleaded guilty and was sentenced to six months in prison. He was also sued by the victim, resulting in the forfeiture of his home. Thankfully, the brass didn't admonish me for failing to dispatch an officer following the initial call.

My first year working at the detachment seemed to fly by, and I was enjoying my new role. It was also evident that the brass thought I was doing a good job when I received my personnel evaluation report, from Staff Sgt. L. J. Jones, who concluded that I made a positive adjustment in my new role and I was …a competent and confident supervisor."

Staff Sgt. Jones's evaluation was reviewed by Insp. E. K. Zalman, who wrote, "I agree with the content of this report. Corporal Ruhl's above-average performance, as shift supervisor is recognized and appreciated. His positive outlook has assisted him in being recommended to compete in the Corporal to Sergeant Process scheduled for November 1984."

SQUAD COMMANDER—DISTRICT 7 CROWD MANAGEMENT UNIT

I entered the competition in November 1984 but wasn't successful. Nevertheless, I was recognized for my leadership abilities and given the position of Commander, District 7 Crowd Management Unit (CMU). The CMU consisted of sixteen officers from district detachments. The members received special training and assisted at various events, including crime scene searches and crowd control. Furthermore, selected members served as pallbearers at police funerals.

The unit met monthly at CFB Borden. The training focused on physical fitness, crowd-control techniques, and gas-gun exercises. We finished with a robust game of floor hockey. (I was the designated goalie.)

I really enjoyed training with the unit, but two incidents left an indelible memory. The first occurred during the gas-gun practice. In this exercise, officers took turns firing the gas gun. Obviously, the projectiles were duds. So, the first officer stepped forward, donned a gas mask, loaded a projectile, and I yelled, "Fire!"

Boom!

"What the fuck?"

A *live* projectile had exploded from the gun, striking the far wall! I was stunned. Why was a live round with the practice rounds? Fortunately, there wasn't gas in the canister. Nevertheless, it was necessary to report the incident to the base commander.

I walked slowly to the base commander's office, all the while wondering how the hell that live shell got in with the practice rounds and what the hell I would say.

I was escorted into his office, where he sat and stared at me from behind a massive desk, with an inscrutable, rock-hard expression on his face. Adrenalin surging, I introduced myself and then, with trepidation, related what had occurred in the gym. When I finished, I expected to be peppered with questions. Instead, and much to my relief, he simply acknowledged it was an accident. Furthermore, he thanked me for reporting the incident and shook my hand. I felt the stress drain from me. I had dodged an explosive bullet.

I also reported the incident to Supt. Burkett. Although he acknowledged the incident was an accident, he thought I should have been more diligent, ensuring all the cartridges were duds, and he recommended I receive remedial training. I never did discover how the projectile got into the same container as the duds.

The second incident was a literal heart stopper. The unit had just finished a five-kilometre run along beautiful Kempenfelt Bay in Barrie. When we were preparing to leave, I noticed an officer draped over the hood of my cruiser. The chap was a bit of a jokester, so I thought he was just fooling around.

"Come on, Bob*," I said with a bit of a chuckle. "We're leaving." When he didn't respond, I looked more closely and could tell he wasn't joking. He appeared lifeless with an ashen pallor.

We put him in my cruiser and raced to the hospital at warp speed. I've been told I'm not the best driver, and that was reinforced when the officer cradling Bob yelled, "Slow down, Dad, or we'll all end up in the hospital!"

When we pulled into the emergency entrance, the hospital staff took over and saved Bob's life. He received a triple bypass and eventually returned to work. This was a wakeup call for management. I submitted a report requesting medical examinations for CMU members, but the request fell on deaf ears.

"DON'T GO, DADDY!"

"Don't go, Daddy!" was the poignant plea uttered by a sorrowful little boy as he watched the lid close on his father's casket. Up until that time, the cadre of macho police officers had managed to keep themselves together in a stoic silence. However, after hearing the little boy's plea, the room erupted in a sea of tears. Len Grove*, a member of the CMU, died following a prolonged battle with cancer. Len was a great guy with a witty sense of humor. I visited him at Mount Sinai Hospital in Toronto, and despite the grave prognosis, he was upbeat. Len related that the tumor was the same kind that ended Terry Fox's life.

I was struck by his candor but saddened when I saw his kid's colourful "Get well, Daddy" drawings next to the bed.

After he returned home, he managed to work around the yard, but members of the Shelburne detachment pitched in when he became incapacitated. Len attended a training session, and the unit presented him with a CMU sweat suit. Eventually, he lost his battle with cancer, and the CMU assembled at his gravesite to perform the OPP flag-folding ceremony. This fastidious exercise involved eight pallbearers—three on each side of the coffin and one each at the head and foot. I was at the foot, and the funeral commander was at the head.

When the members assembled, I uttered two commands. The first was to remove the band securing the Ontario flag. "Remove band!" I released the band and was handing it to the pallbearer next to me when it slipped out of my hands, flew along the casket, and was skillfully caught by the funeral commander. (I wondered if Len was watching from above and chuckling.) My second command was "Fold flag!" The officers took turns maintaining a tight triangular configuration until it reached the funeral commander, who presented it to Len's widow. It was a fitting tribute to an officer and a gentleman. Rest in peace, Len.

THE MAPLE STREET BRAWL

One of the things that makes police work interesting is the uncertainty. One minute you're minding your own business, and the next you're up to your ass in alligators.

On a summer evening in 1990, Pat and I were picking up Jeff and his friend from the movie theatre in downtown Barrie. I parked on Maple Street, and we walked to the theatre to meet the kids.

On our return, I spotted a pickup truck back into our car and then prepared to take off. I ran to the truck and saw that both occupants were wearing vests adorned with skull and crossbones and FTW (Fuck the World) patches, so I assumed they were outlaw bikers. The driver rolled down the window and looked at me as if to say "What?"

"You just hit my car!" I said. "Get out. We need to talk!" The driver glared at me while the passenger leaned toward the driver's window.

"Have you ever done hard time, buddy?" he asked.

"Yeah," I replied without thinking. "Now get out!"

Pat overheard the conversation and, anticipating a confrontation, searched for anything I could use as a weapon. Finding nothing and fearing for my safety, she sent Jeff and his friend to the Roxx, a local bar around the corner, to get help.

When the driver exited the vehicle, he was obviously impaired. I identified myself as a police officer and placed him under arrest. I wasn't sure if the passenger heard me, so I told him I was a cop, and his buddy was under arrest. "You can't arrest him; you're wearing shorts," he replied, uncomfortably close to me.

"Get out of my face!" I yelled.

Meanwhile, Pat had called the OPP and told them to contact the Barrie police because I needed help.

The passenger was still in my face, so I pushed him back, and he lunged at me. I took a swing but missed. At that moment, Jeff turned to his mom. "Doesn't Dad know how to fight?"

My second attempt was a haymaker, and the biker fell backwards, then jumped up and took off running as two bouncers from the Roxx chased him. The Barrie police still hadn't arrived, so Pat called the OPP again.

Meanwhile, the driver tried to run. Pat grabbed his shirt, but he broke free. I noticed a guy standing at the corner of Maple and Dunlop Streets and shouted to him. "I'm with the OPP! Grab that guy!" The bystander stuck out his foot and tripped him. I took the biker into custody.

A short time later, the two burly bouncers returned carrying the passenger, who by then was missing his front teeth. A subsequent investigation revealed the two bikers had lengthy criminal records. Furthermore, when I searched their truck, I discovered a butcher knife stashed above the sun visor. Ironically, the passenger was arrested for impaired driving a couple of weeks later. Not surprisingly, the arresting officer required backup to affect the arrest. In a rather humorous aside, he was at the detachment for fingerprinting when I was present. "I think you've already met, Sergeant Ruhl," the arresting officer said.

You never know what you'll run into when you're wearing shorts.

COINCIDENCE

I was enjoying my new duties and not thinking about Larry Talbot until I read a newspaper article on Saturday, January 8, 1994. The headline in the *Toronto Star* was riveting, "Six Slayings May Be Linked." The article went on to say that "The unsolved sex slayings of six women in southern Ontario show a number of striking similarities suggesting the murders are linked." The victims included: Jenny Isford, Christine Prince, Delia Adriano, Valerie Stevens, Lynda Shaw, and Cindy Halliday. All the women had been kidnapped and taken to remote areas, where they were murdered. The homicides occurred during early spring and late summer. (Isford and Shaw were solved. The remaining are cold cases.)

CINDY HALLIDAY

Cindy Halliday was last seen hitchhiking on April 20, 1992, near the village of Midhurst. She was returning to her home in Waverley, a village northeast of Elmvale. Her body was discovered in a reforestation area near Horseshoe Valley Road (County Rd 22 and Township Rd 2) about 10 km north of where she was last seen hitchhiking. At the time, Larry Talbot was living in Gravenhurst, 75 km north of where her body was found. (On July 18, 1993, Talbot was ticketed for speeding on County Rd 22 by an officer from my platoon.)

On January 14, 1994, I sent a report to Det. Insp. Barry Thompson, the lead investigator in the Halliday homicide. I included the report I had submitted previously that persuaded the brass to implement Project Tree. The correspondence included Talbot's address and the speeding ticket he received on July 18, 1993, on County Road 22. I recommended that he should be considered a person of interest in the Halliday homicide. Insp. Thompson didn't contact me. However, my next-door neighbor said he was at a party with Chief Supt. Wayne Frechette, who wanted me to know he was investigating Talbot. He also learned from Frechette that two "hitchhikers" (undercover cops) had been deployed to entice Talbot but were unsuccessful. What a difference ten years and a change in command made. A decade after Project Tree was scrapped, Talbot was once again a person of interest. I never learned what his status was in terms of the investigation.

OFFICER DOWN

I was exposed to many perilous and even life-threatening situations during my career, but thankfully, apart from the pellet gun incident with Talbot, I had never experienced the terror of being shot. I think it safe to say that most police officers, whether they admit it or not, have thought about the possibility of being shot.

Unfortunately, on a summer night in 1992, this became a reality for a member of my platoon. In the early morning hours of June 29, 1992, two men shot and killed a young man in the Bracebridge area and then fled in the victim's truck. Unaware that the occupants had murdered a man less than an hour before, Constable Scott Couse pulled the vehicle over for speeding. When he approached the driver's side, the driver said, "Good evening officer," and then shot Scott! He managed to flee across Highway 400, and a passerby called for assistance. Scott was rushed to the nearby hospital, and his prognosis was good. (The suspects were arrested the following day in Hamilton.)

CRITICAL INCIDENT STRESS DEBRIEFING (CISD)

I was awakened by a frantic call from a dispatcher at the Barrie comm. centre. He advised that Scott had been shot during a traffic stop and was in stable condition. The call shocked me to the core, and I tried to make sense of the horrific news. Who shot him? How did it happen? Where did it happen? I was also feeling guilty for not being on duty. Prior to Scott's shooting, I had been trained as a peer support provider (PSP). PSPs are experienced in assisting officers who are struggling with emotional issues. They also assist the force psychologist during critical incident stress debriefings (CISD), so I was selected to assist a psychologist conducting a CISD for the officers on duty the night of the shooting.

When I arrived at the detachment, I noticed some somber officers mingling in small groups trying to make sense of the shooting. I met with the psychologist, and we decided to hold a CISD that evening. I was feeling somewhat concerned about assisting in the CISD. After all, I was the platoon supervisor, and I was worried the participants may not feel comfortable sharing with their supervisor present. When the CISD commenced, I introduced the psychologist and told the officers the following: "This debriefing is not just about what happened to Scott. Rather, it is about how Scott's shooting has affected us. This is an opportunity to share your thoughts and feelings in a safe setting. The psychologist will help you understand the reactions you may be experiencing because of this event. It's important to understand that we are committed to confidentiality. So, anything that is said in the room stays in the room. The psychologist will ask you questions to facilitate the debriefing, but if you don't want to participate, simply say 'pass.' However, you may assist others by sharing your thoughts and feelings. Are there any questions?"

I now realize that by being a peer supporter, I was unable to benefit from the debriefing because I had thoughts and feelings about the shooting that I couldn't share. Essentially, my task was to provide support but not receive support. When a police officer is shot, members contend with the realization that it could happen to them. Spouses and family members also come to terms with that same frightening realization. Prior to Scott's shooting, whenever a police officer was killed or injured, there was little thought about the fears and concerns of officers' families. Ultimately, the spouses would either get together to discuss their fears or were left alone to grapple with them. Consequently, we decided to offer a support debriefing for family members too. It was well attended, and the attendees seemed grateful for the opportunity to participate.

Whenever a police officer is shot the level of anxiety rises significantly. Following Scott's shooting, many members altered their "vehicle stop" tactics. I recall patrolling with an officer and instead of going to the driver's door, we approached the passenger door. Essentially, Scott's ambush reinforced the notion that there are bad guys who could kill us.

Scott was an inspiration. When he returned to work, he was offered a desk job as part of the process of transitioning back to patrol duties. He declined and returned to the platoon. When I think of the anxiety, I experienced stopping cars after Scott's shooting, I can't imagine the courage it took for him to approach vehicles when he returned to work. Scott eventually became a member of the Critical Incident Peer Support Team. He spoke to recruit classes at the OPP academy, emphasizing the necessity to remain vigilant during vehicle stops and extolling the benefits of peer and/or professional support should officers ever be involved in a critical incident.

END OF WATCH

Tom Coffin wasn't as fortunate as Scott Couse. On April 24, 1996, Constable Coffin, stationed at the Midland detachment, charged the chair of the Penetanguishene Police Services Board with impaired driving. Following the arrest, the chair threatened to kill Constable Coffin.

On May 31, 1997, Constable Coffin was enjoying a drink with his colleagues at a local bar when he was shot in the back of the head.

The news is never good when the phone rings in the middle of the night. And the news of Cst. Coffin's murder was an incredible shock. I assisted OPP Psychologist Dr. David Hoath, conducting a series of CISDs with officers and family members. This was the end of watch for a well-respected officer, who was survived by his wife and three young children. Rest in peace, Provincial Constable Tom Coffin.

NEW HORIZONS, NEW GOALS

I was fifty years old and anxiously awaiting retirement. I was also looking forward to a second career as an addiction counsellor for the OPP. Several months earlier, I had approached Dr. David Hoath with the proposal. He concurred, and it was approved by the command staff. Essentially, I'd be seconded to the Human Resources Branch. Nevertheless, retirement was several months away, and I was still on the road and feeling anxious after Scott's shooting, I was also troubled when I read about a New York City police officer who was shot and killed within hours of retiring.

My apprehension peaked when I attended a pre-retirement seminar where Dr. Hoath was a speaker. He mentioned that it was common for officers to become quite anxious prior to retiring. He cited the following. Imagine, your family is going on a holiday to Aruba. However, you're scheduled to work midnights on the Friday night/Saturday morning of your trip. You report for duty. So, what are you thinking? You're thinking about the much-anticipated vacation, but you fear that it won't happen if you're injured or killed. So, what do you do? You patrol the isolated side roads that haven't seen traffic for years. If that is true, he posited, how anxious are officers still on the road prior to retirement?

I rode "shotgun" with members of the platoon. Nevertheless, I was "wounded" by a horrific crime before the curtain came down on my career.

MURDEROUS INFATUATION

There's an aspect of policing that I never got used to: death investigations. During my career, I encountered the grim reaper on many occasions, but I managed to avoid the distinction of being the first officer at a murder scene. That was about to change months before I retired.

I was enjoying a quiet drive through Midhurst, a quaint village eight kilometres west of Barrie. I have many fond memories of Midhurst. When I was transferred to Barrie, Pat and I were house hunting and discovered Midhurst, replete with forests, nature trails, wildlife, and woodland streams. We fell in love with the bounty that Mother Nature had bestowed on the village and purchased a home there. It was a peaceful community where a typical police call involved barking dogs or the odd noise complaint. That changed when I received an ominous call from the comm. centre.

The dispatcher requested I check an abandoned vehicle at Willow Creek in Midhurst. When I arrived, a late-model Ford was parked on the shoulder. I was about to search the area when the dispatcher requested, I call the comm. centre from my residence, because the public were monitoring our calls. I called the comm. centre and was advised a physiotherapist from a Barrie clinic had reported a co-worker failed to report for work. She lived on Finley Mill Road near my residence.

When I arrived, I spoke to an individual who was very agitated. He said the woman was a co-worker at the Cedar Rehabilitation Clinic. He called her residence, but no one answered. Alarmed, he went to her house, and when he saw her vehicle, he thought she was home. But when he knocked, no one answered, so he opened the unlocked door and called for her. Silence. He thought it was odd, so he searched the home but couldn't locate her. Finally, he decided to check the basement. He paused momentarily and began sobbing and blurted out that he had spotted her lifeless body propped against the clothes dryer. Horrified, he called the police.

I entered the residence, my senses electrified. I walked slowly down the steps into the basement, and then I spotted her. She was propped against the clothes dryer and had been shot in the chest and stabbed multiple times. Her eyes were still open, as if staring at me. I will never be able to forget that gruesome scene.

I contacted the comm. centre and requested backup. When the officers arrived, they moved onlookers from the area and roped off the perimeter of the residence. I assigned an officer to record vehicles driving past the residence. (In some instances, perpetrators return to the crime scene.) Another officer was responsible for noting the names and times officials entered and left the residence. When a detective inspector arrived from the Criminal Investigation Branch, I updated him on the preliminary investigation.

The subsequent investigation revealed, the twenty-one-year-old shooter was a client at the clinic and became infatuated with the victim. He gifted her with a mountain bike a week prior to the homicide. However, she wasn't interested in a relationship with him. Consequently, he murdered her and then returned to Willow Creek, where he shot himself in the head. We discovered his body and a shotgun in the middle of a shallow creek.

When I returned home, I painted our basement walls white. I think it served to momentarily distract me from the thoughts and emotions I was experiencing. Nevertheless, I cannot eradicate the horrible memory of the young woman's untimely demise.

PART 3

BOOZE AFTER THE BADGE

CHAPTER 8
ADDICTION COUNSELLOR

If you want others to be happy, practice compassion.
If you want to be happy, practice compassion.

– *The Dalai Lama*

WHEN I WAS GIVEN THE opportunity to reach out to officers who were struggling with substance abuse, my mission was to enlighten them, so they would avoid the self-destructive journey I had endured. A social work degree that I had obtained at York University in 1995 was an asset, but the "university of hard knocks" also prepped me for the role.

The morning of my calling, I awoke feeling uneasy, thinking, *What the hell have I got myself into?* I stared at the ceiling wondering how the rank and file would react to a retired cop lecturing to them on the evils of drinking. After all, I was no longer one of them. Conversely, I wondered how I'd react if they derided my role with dismissive comments like "Bullshit" and "Who do you think you are?" I reinforced my resolve with a personal mission statement: "Tell my story to those who will listen and respond with compassion and understanding to those who show a desire to ask for help."

The drive to OPP GHQ afforded me an opportunity to mull over the pushback I might receive from the naysayers. Why was I engaged in stinky thinking? I had learned at the Donwood that it was self-defeating. Alcoholics who go down that rabbit hole convince themselves they'll likely fail. First, they say to themselves, "I knew it; I knew I would fail." Next, because they "predicted" their failure, it reinforces their negative self-image. Finally, it often affords the alcoholic a reason to drink with self-defeating statements like "I might as well drink; I'm a failure, anyway." But what happens to those who are successful? They don't take credit for their success, saying instead that the task was easy and, therefore, of no value. Or they become arrogant and boastful, overcompensating for their poor self-image.

Consequently, I replaced negative self-talk with an optimistic outlook: *I have no evidence to support my belief that I will be spurned and rejected. I'm an experienced and respected retired police officer, and the OPP have expressed confidence by accepting me for the addiction counsellor position. I have no idea what the future will entail, but I'm going to do my very best.*

When I arrived at OPP GHQ, I reported to the Human Resources Branch (HRB), where I met Staff Sergeant Terry Kidd.[32] Terry was a good-natured fellow who had recently transferred to GHQ. He welcomed me with a broad smile and a robust handshake. He also took me under his wing and introduced me to the rest of the HR staff. I was eager to begin.

JUST THE FACTS

Based on my experience, I knew alcohol abuse was rampant in the law-enforcement community. (Historically, booze has been the "special guest" at stags, promotional parties, golf tournaments, funerals, and shift parties.) So, I designed a presentation that underscored the insidious risks of abusing alcohol. I also included my enduring battle to establish street cred with the students. When I showed the presentation to my supervisor, Dr. David Hoath, he thought some slides were too busy and somewhat confusing. Yikes! That wasn't what I wanted to hear. So, I burned the midnight oil revising it. When we met again, I was a tad nervous, hoping it would pass the "Hoath test." I was relieved when he arrived with coffee and doughnuts, an obvious throwback to his policing days in Toronto. The revision passed the test, and I was good to go!

It wasn't long before managers were contacting me when they suspected officers of alcohol-related performance deficiencies. I also spoke to the gung-ho recruits at the OPP academy in Brampton. I knew some recruits were probably prone to abusing alcohol and might see themselves in me. However, I suspected my message would likely fall on deaf ears. I could imagine a younger version of myself in the class saying, "Not me! That will never happen to me."

---

32 Sadly, Terry passed away from kidney cancer a couple of years later. He was posthumously awarded the rank of inspector, a deserving recognition for an officer and a gentleman.

ARE YOU ONE OF US?

Police officers, like soldiers, rely on each other for support and safety. To a large extent, officers patrol alone. Consequently, when the call "Officer needs assistance" is broadcast, cops, race to the scene. Every cop is aware that the next call for help could come from them. So, all hands- on deck! An unspoken bond exists among officers that defies race, gender, religion, and sexual orientation. This extends beyond on-duty hours too. So, if the shift has a "choir practice,"[33] everyone, including rookies, is expected to attend. To decline leaves everyone questioning the rookie's loyalty. "Can this guy/gal really be trusted?" I discussed the conundrum and acknowledged that off-duty gatherings were often helpful in maintaining esprit de corps, but I added that if a rookie, didn't want to participate, he or she might cave due to peer pressure. Although many students believed peer pressure might be an issue, most thought they could make the ultimate decision. But I knew when the rubber hit the road, the recruits would face a formidable foe: the shift!

STRESS MANAGEMENT

I also introduced stress management and the use of alcohol and identified the variables that cause stress and how it can cause sleeplessness, physiological tension, and interpersonal problems. I talked about the causal relationship of self-medicating to reduce tension and briefly escape from the memories of tragic investigations that may be haunting them.

I shared an anecdote involving an officer who was advised his young son had died from a protracted battle with cancer. As you can imagine, the officer was devastated when he left the detachment. I felt sorry for him and his family. A senior shift member said, "We've got to get him drunk!" Many recruits thought the suggestion was inappropriate. However, I knew from experience that this was normative behaviour in some situations. It also underscored the fact that alcohol played a significant role in police culture because it acted as a quick fix after officers were exposed to tragedies and feelings of helplessness. Essentially, self-medication enabled officers to suppress, avoid, and deny disturbing work-related memories, thoughts, and feelings, at least in the short term.

I shared with the students some coping strategies associated with the five domains of personal well-being: physical (nutrition, exercise, proper rest), cognitive (being aware of

---

33   The term "choir practice" was coined by Joseph Wambaugh in his book *The Choirboys*, referring to getting together after shift to drink and party.

negative cognitive distortions), emotional (learning to accurately label and express one's feelings and emotions), social (establishing and maintaining close intimate relationships and at least one trusted relationship), and spiritual (a core set of optimistic beliefs, values, and principles). These are the pillars that maintain structure, purpose, and meaning in one's life.

BEWARE OF THE "BOOZYMAN"

I completed my presentation by showing the recruits a photograph of me when I was hungover. The picture underscored the downside of excessive boozing—the morning after.

Presenting to a recruit class
(Credit: Barry Ruhl)

The photograph was taken following an evening of excessive drinking at the Breslau Hotel. On Monday evenings, the shift gathered at the watering hole because it featured steak "on the cheap!" The trade-off was the pricey tab for pitchers of draft beer. Many pitchers later, and after few hours of sleep, "Boozy Barry" was expected to report for duty regardless of the hangover.

On one such morning as I entered the detachment, my supervisor instructed me to report to the Identification Unit because I required a new photograph for my warrant card.

I attempted to appear as un-hungover as possible. Nevertheless, anyone looking at my visage could tell I was one hurting puppy.

I asked the recruits what they thought about the picture. Silence. Either they didn't realize I was hungover, they were being polite, or they were too frightened to say anything. After a few moments, I continued. "I showed you the picture to illustrate what a hangover looks like. Can anyone see anything that would indicate I was hungover?" A few recruits said my eyes appeared bloodshot, and a few noted my flat, lifeless facial expression. I agreed and added that it is difficult to put on a happy face when your head is pounding like a runaway jackhammer. I finished by emphasizing that out-of-control drinking could have serious consequences. "Don't let the Boozyman get you!"

I'M HERE FOR YOU

In addition to my responsibilities as an educator, I also assisted supervisors when members were struggling with substance abuse that was affecting their work. I was pleasantly surprised when they reached out shortly after my arrival. I reasoned that my thirty-year career enhanced my credibility. Nevertheless, few officers with issues were knocking on my door. They essentially coped by living a SAD life; that is, a tendency to *suppress, avoid*, and *deny*. However, I was able to assist several officers. I've included two such interventions below but altered the stories to protect their privacy.

"I THINK I NEED YOUR HELP"

In August 1996, I received a call from a staff sgt. in southern Ontario. Two officers had detected alcohol on a member's breath, and he was sent home. He had previously been disciplined for testifying while "mildly inebriated." Despite that infraction, he continued to drink on duty. The staff sgt. was going to meet with the officer and wanted my advice. I suggested that he name the inappropriate behaviour and the possibility there would be serious consequences if it continued. I also asked him to mention that I was available to assist him.

The officer called me the next day. He accepted that he needed help and said, "I think I need your services." He described his downward boozy spiral and his unsuccessful attempts at quitting. He was concerned that his drinking was affecting his work performance, and his spouse was threatening to leave him. It sounded like he was motivated, so I recommended the Bellwood addiction program because several officers had experienced successful outcomes there. I also gave him the name of a peer supporter who had completed the program. He reiterated that he wanted to quit drinking. He talked the talk, but I wondered if he would walk the walk.

A week later, he contacted the Bellwood and was waiting for an admittance date. However, his desire went south when he was observed driving into the detachment and reported for duty with alcohol on his breath. His supervisor demanded a breath sample and the readings were over .08. He was charged with operating a motor vehicle with a blood alcohol level above .08. I received the troubling news from his supervisor, who allowed me to speak to him. I suggested that he contact the Bellwood because the program had an accelerated admittance policy based on emergency circumstances. I also suggested that he enter a detoxification facility in case he experienced severe withdrawal symptoms, including headaches, anxiety, and tremors.

A few days later, the officer called from a detox facility. He related that the first few days had been challenging, but they reinforced his resolve to enter the Bellwood. I encouraged him to stay strong *one day at a time*.

The officer completed the Bellwood program, and his wife stayed with him and joined a support group. He pleaded guilty to the Criminal Code charge but didn't lose his job. He was on the road to recovery and joined an aftercare program and attended Alcoholic Anonymous meetings. I was happy for him, recalling how great I felt when I finally achieved sobriety. We exchanged goodbyes, and I wished him every success in the future. I also reminded him that I was a phone call away. He maintained his sobriety and eventually became a proud member of the OPP Peer Support Program.

BOOZE CAN KILL

Unfortunately, other officers couldn't remain abstinent. In February 1995, a staff sgt. in northern Ontario contacted me when an officer reported for duty with alcohol on his breath. The staff sgt. confronted the officer, who readily admitted that he had a drinking problem and volunteered to seek treatment immediately. However, he left the program after a few days. The detachment commander believed he had enrolled in the program simply to avoid being disciplined. I mused that he would likely be a disciplinary challenge and a morale buster at the detachment if he continued to drink. I suggested he meet with the elusive officer, underscore the inappropriateness of reporting for duty with alcohol on his breath, and order him to complete the program.

When they met, the staff sgt. asked him why he left the program. The officer said he didn't like sharing information with a "bunch of rounders" during group therapy, and the counsellor had "unjustly accused" him of being verbally aggressive during the sessions. The staff sgt. asked what he was going to do about the drinking. He replied that *he didn't have a drinking problem!* He also said he regretted telling the staff sgt. that he had a problem, believing he was simply "depressed." The staff sgt. ordered him to re-enter treatment and cautioned that if he refused, an Employee Referral Procedure (ERP) would be submitted. (The ERP named the circumstances of reporting for duty with alcohol on his breath and refusing to return to treatment when requested to do so.)

The officer must have thought the staff sgt. was serious and applied for a re-entry date. He was also attending AA meetings. I called the staff sgt. for an update, and he thought the officer appeared to be motivated. But I knew from my history with booze, it was too easy to fall off the wagon. Unfortunately, the officer relapsed following a meeting with the director at the treatment facility. So, the staff sgt. warned him that disciplinary action would be considered if he didn't enter a treatment program. Consequently, he enlisted in the Bellwood program.

The officer completed the program and was transferred to another district. I periodically checked on his progress and learned he had relapsed. I was concerned he could be riding on the boozy slippery slope. That reality hit home when he was killed in a single-vehicle crash after leaving a bar. The officer's body was discovered the following morning at the bottom of a steep ravine. This was tragic and caused me to recall the many occasions I had driven impaired, but miraculously survived!

CHAPTER 9

YOU HAVE PROSTATE CANCER

> Bottle of wine, fruit of the vine,
> When you gonna let me get sober.
> Leave me alone, let me go home.
> I wanna go back and start over.
>
> *– Tom Paxton*

IN NOVEMBER 1995, MY DOCTOR discovered a lumpy growth on my prostate during my annual physical. When I left his office, my head was reeling!

A week later, I underwent a prostate biopsy and waited in excruciating anxiety for the results. I spent countless hours ruminating about the future. Absent the results, I thought I had cancer and was on my deathbed. I fretted about Pat and Jeff's future when I was gone. Who would look after them? Furthermore, I was wallowing in the unfairness of it all. I had survived chasing bad guys for decades, only to face a possible death sentence.

On the day of reckoning, the doctor's solemn demeanor prepared me for the worst. "Barry," he began, "I'm sorry, the laboratory results indicate you have a tumor." I was gobsmacked! He said he would contact a colleague at Oakville's Trafalgar-Memorial Hospital to arrange a consultation.

Pat and I met Dr. Richard Casey two weeks later. I was immediately impressed by his compassionate manner. He explained that the tumor was on the outer layer of the prostate gland and hadn't metastasized. He recommended I enroll in an eight-month clinical trial before removing it. He explained the trial was to determine the efficacy of Lupron in lowering testosterone levels, which has a significant effect on tumorous cell growth. Pat, who had been quiet, asked Dr. Casey what would have happened if the tumor had not been discovered. His reply was ominous. "Within five years, Barry would have been in serious trouble!" Alarmed, I wanted it gone! But Dr. Casey recommended leaving the "little shit" alone for another eight months! What if it spread? Then, I'd be in big trouble! Pat and I discussed the alternatives but decided to follow Dr. Casey's recommendation. However, I could not stop worrying that the tumor might metastasize.

For the next eight months, I received Lupron injections monthly and was encouraged by the results. My testosterone levels decreased, and the tumor shrank. But during this tense interlude, I learned that the Canadian Red Cross had infected thousands of people with HIV and Hepatitis C with tainted blood. There was no bloody way I was taking a chance, so I banked four litres of blood for the operation.

> Success is not final; failure is not fatal:
> It is the courage to continue that counts.
>
> *– Winston Churchill*

"So, I have cancer, and it could kill me" was the mantra that preoccupied my thoughts following the diagnosis. I was scared shit-less and wasted countless hours ruminating about the "what ifs." I knew stinky thinking was counterproductive, so I focused on the positives. I accepted that if the surgery was unsuccessful, radiation and chemotherapy were viable alternatives. I reviewed articles on prostate cancer that helped eradicate the "what ifs." I also resumed physical exercise, which helped relieve stress. I enlisted our two-year old Labrador retriever, Ruhler, to be my "trainer." Her puppyish antics helped me feel upbeat. I recall Ruhler waiting for me, tongue dangling and tail wagging so forcefully that she could have cleared a table. I also surfed the Internet for information on nutrition and learned that antioxidants may protect cells from free radicals (molecules that can damage cells). I also discovered the Mediterranean Diet, which includes foods that contain antioxidants. So, Pat and I visited a local supermarket and filled our shopping cart with "Mediterranean" foods.

REUNION WITH THE BOOZYMAN

I had a healthy regime in terms of nutritional needs and exercise. Nevertheless, I continued to search for anything that would augment my anti-cancer arsenal. I was watching a TV documentary in December 1995 and was fascinated by a program that extolled the benefits of drinking red wine. Grape skins contain resveratrol, a powerful antioxidant that neutralizes free radicals believed to be a factor in aging.[34] So, rejecting Pat's insistence that I could be jeopardizing my sobriety, I drank two glasses of red wine daily—even though I could have acquired antioxidants by consuming non-alcoholic grape juice! I still recall the warm rush and Little Barry saying, "Welcome home."

Soon, two glasses became four, and as my tolerance increased, four became the bottle. I was reporting for work hungover and aware that I was a hypocrite, preaching to students about alcohol abuse while getting wasted! But I never considered quitting.

SHOWTIME

On June 28, 1996, I was admitted to the Oakville Trafalgar-Memorial Hospital. Dr. Casey dropped in and discussed the pending surgery, including the fact I had a small prostate gland. Gladdened by the news, I responded, "Hey, that sounds great, Dr. Casey!"

Wrong!

"You see, Barry," he said, "your prostate is so small, I'll have a difficult time handling it."

What? No! TMI! I didn't need to hear that! I couldn't banish the frightening image of Dr. Casey's hands fumbling with my small prostate.

On the morning of the surgery, my spirits were lifted when I was awakened by a call from Lynn Hoath, (Dr. Hoath's wife), wishing me good luck and praying for a speedy recovery. Showtime!

I was wheeled through many vacant corridors and finally into the operating theatre. It resembled a scene from the *Twilight Zone* because the surgical team appeared to be wearing spacesuits. One of them greeted me with a cheery "Good morning, Barry." It was Dr. Casey.

"I hope everyone had a good night's sleep," I replied nervously.

---

34   https://www.drugs.com/resveratrol.html

Following the cheerful banter, the anesthetic kicked in, and it was sleepy time. I awoke following surgery feeling like I had been gutted. When the anesthetic cleared, I experienced excruciating pain.

Later that day, Dr. Casey visited, grinning like a Cheshire cat. The operation had been a success, and a lab analysis confirmed that the tumor hadn't metastasized. Great news indeed. He thought I could be released in a few days and suggested I take brief walks in the meantime. So, I frequently walked the hospital corridors kibitzing with other "walking wounded." I was feeling much better and after three days was ready to go home. But there was a "small" problem. We had a Volkswagen and I required a larger vehicle so I could lie down. Showing admirable initiative, Pat called Supt. Burkett, and he assigned an officer to transport me home in a station wagon.

The post-operative period was challenging for Pat and me. During my recovery, Pat's mother was being treated for terminal stomach cancer. It was difficult watching her care for my needs while also supporting her mother.

I visited the hospital monthly to track my prostate specific antigen (PSA) levels. (PSA is a protein created by the prostate gland and a marker for prostate cancer.) Post-surgery PSA levels are expected to reach undetectable levels within six to eight weeks. If the levels didn't drop, there is a possibility that cancerous cells are still present. Imagine how I was feeling when the levels didn't decline quickly. In fact, it was eighteen months before my PSA levels were undetectable. A welcome relief indeed. Nevertheless, the levels are still checked yearly. According to the National Cancer Institute of Canada, one in twenty-seven men died of prostate cancer in 1996.[35] When I revisit this time in my life, I realize I was extremely fortunate and blessed to have Pat at my side.

HOLA, CUBA

In February 1997, Pat and I decided we needed a holiday. I had recovered from surgery and was feeling well enough to travel. So, Cuba, here we come! The all-inclusive five-star resort was in Varadero, about 140 km east of Havana, and we had picked a winner. The buildings were luxurious, the pools magnificent, and the grounds were adorned with lush palm trees. It also had a private beach with soft white sand and a tiki bar, just what Little Barry needed.

---

35   https://www.cancer.gov/

Soon after arriving, we learned the staff earned subsistence wages, so I palmed the maître d' and waiters a few US dollars. Not surprisingly, we were extended first-class service. (Tipping, in US dollars was somewhat tricky because it was illegal for Cubans to possess US currency. In future visits to the island, we brought toiletries, analgesics, and vitamins for the staff.) "Muchas Gracias Senor" was a wonderful salutation from the grateful staff.

DINING AT A PALADAR

A "paladar" is a restaurant operated by families and directed at tourists seeking a more vivid interaction with Cuban reality and looking for homemade Cuban food.[36] We lucked out when Juan, the maître d' at the restaurant, invited us to his home for dinner. It seemed like a wonderful opportunity to experience Cuban culture. So, that evening we were driven to Juan's in an iconic 1957 Chevrolet! Our driver was quite chatty, identifying places of interest along the Gulf coast.

Suddenly, I noticed a distinct change in the surroundings. Instead of the quaint streets and gorgeous Spanish architecture, the streets were littered with garbage, and many of the homes had seen better days. When we arrived at Juan's, we wondered if we had made the right decision. After a brief discussion, and feeling somewhat uneasy, we cautiously climbed the creaky steps.

I knocked on the dilapidated door not knowing what to expect. However, when it opened, we were greeted by Juan and his smiling parents, Maria and Alfredo. It was the beginning of a wonderful evening, and it wasn't long before we were conversing like old friends. We learned that Alfredo (who looked much older than his sixty-five years) had been the executive manager of an exclusive hotel in Varadero. Unfortunately, Fidel Castro or the "big guy," as Alfredo called him, terminated him when he reached sixty-five. He was replaced by a member of "the Party." It was apparent he was using "rum therapy" as a means of coping with the draconian decision. Remarkably, he drank a full forty-pounder without offering me a sip.

Maria was a friendly, engaging woman who recalled their luxurious lifestyle. She regaled us with a vivid description of their spacious home overlooking the Gulf of Mexico. It was obvious she was saddened by the loss of their previous lifestyle.

36   https://en.wikipedia.org/wiki/Paladar

Eventually, Maria announced dinner was served. Despite the meagre surroundings, the meal included freshly squeezed orange juice, jumbo shrimp, brown rice, and plantains. As we enjoyed the delicious offerings, I thought it was unfortunate that the family relied on tourists to supplement their income.

When it was time to say goodbye, I palmed Maria some money and thanked her for the enjoyable evening. We reminisced about our memorable night while returning to the resort and laughed at our apprehension prior to meeting the heartwarming family. Ironically, the visit with Alfredo's family was the highlight of our holiday.

HELP!

We were lounging on the beach a couple of days before leaving the resort. I was hungover and still feeling tipsy. because the previous evening I once again overindulged, much to Little Barry's delight! So, I thought a dip in the Gulf might sober me up. However, there was a rather glaring problem because the red flag was warning people of undertows. Did I pay heed to the ominous notice? Hell no! I was an excellent swimmer, so I jumped into the surf and swam feverishly away from shore. The turquoise tropical waters were soothing as I floated effortlessly on my back thinking, *Life is good*. It was an exhilarating experience watching the seagulls gliding aimlessly overhead, and I didn't have a worry in the world.

Wrong!

Beginning to tire, I decided to head to shore, only to discover I wasn't moving. What the hell? I tried again using powerful strokes and flutter kicks. Again, I wasn't any closer to the shore. Shit! I was in big trouble! I realized I was trapped in a riptide and hitting the proverbial "wall," and I was exhausted! Inexplicably, I was overcome by a sense of calmness. I surrendered to the treacherous waters, thinking, s*o, this is how it ends*. Panic and my will to survive were replaced by a grim realization: *I'm going to drown!* I descended into a profound sadness thinking of Pat and Jeff and realizing I would no longer be there for them.

At that moment, I glanced toward the shore and spotted someone waving. Relieved, I returned his wave. Much to my dismay, he began walking away. *God, he probably thinks I'm OK*, I thought.

"Help! Help!" I screamed, frantically waving my arms. Luckily, he glanced in my direction and then rushed into the surf. Realizing help was on the way, I was imbued with hope. Nevertheless, I was struggling to stay afloat, and it seemed like an eternity before my saviour arrived. "Hurry, hurry, don't give up, don't give up," became my survival mantra.

Where is he? Suddenly, I heard a voice in broken English, "I save you." He took hold of me and swam parallel to the shoreline before changing direction and heading to shore. When we reached the beach, I was exhausted. The overwhelming feelings of relief caused me to embrace my hero. (When I calmed down, I realized he was the same individual I spotted chatting up bikini-clad women when we arrived at the beach. Of course, my cynical cop side emerged, and I commented to Pat, "There's a dude with nothing to do but chat up the chicks." Wrong!)

Pat was immersed in a John Jakes novel when I exclaimed, "Pat, I nearly fucking drowned!" She looked up from her book. "Barry, watch your language. People will hear you!"

"Did you not hear me? I almost drowned!"

She looked me over. "Oh, my goodness, are you OK?" Suffice to say, Racile, my hero, wouldn't need to shop at the ration store for quite some time!

The author and his saviour, Racile
(Credit: Barry Ruhl)

Before leaving the resort, I obsessed about my near-death experience. I was a peer supporter, so I realized I was probably experiencing post-traumatic stress. In addition to repeatedly reliving the near-death experience, my mind was flooded with questions, such as, "What if Racile hadn't seen me?" "What would it feel like to drown?" "What if my body wasn't found?" and "What would life be like for Pat and Jeff without me?" I realized it had been a big mistake to ignore the caution flags. I also had to face the grim reality that my over-the-top drinking was a factor in the errant behavior.

A few days later, we were flying home, and I realized that I was lucky that my final resting place wasn't in the Gulf of Mexico. So, when the beverage cart rolled down the aisle, I ordered a Diet Coke and renewed my commitment to jump back on the wagon. But would it last?

A DRY LANDING

When I returned home, I remained abstinent. My near-death experience was a wake-up call. I relived frightening nightmares about it, awakening drenched in sweat! (I'm still hyper-cautious when I go swimming, and when my grandchildren are with me, I'm "Cranky Pop Pop" constantly reminding them to stay closer to shore.) When Little Barry attempted to "open the bar," I recalled the near-death experience and enjoy a Diet Coke. I also managed to keep Little Barry at bay when I was busy assisting officers battling substance abuse.

ALL GOOD THINGS COME TO AN END

I was the OPP addiction counsellor from 1994–1998. It was a privilege for me to be able to assist members with substance abuse issues, and it was gratifying to receive a letter of commendation from Commissioner Tom O'Grady. The commendation read, in part, …I acknowledge, appreciate, and commend you for your success, in dealing with the most private and difficult personal crises faced by members and their families." Now, I was embarking on my third career, retirement.

CHAPTER 10

WASTED DAYS AND WASTED NIGHTS

*Addiction is a special kind of Hell.
It takes the soul of the addict and
breaks the hearts of everyone who loves them.*

– Addiction Today

IN 1999, WE LEFT MIDHURST and relocated to Southampton on the eastern shores of Lake Huron. Pat invited her brother, Rob, and his family to join us for Thanksgiving. It has always been a favorite holiday for Pat. She loved preparing the festive dinner: stuffing the bird, mashing the potatoes, and baking her delicious pumpkin pie. She also enjoyed decorating our century-old home with rustic colours and plump pumpkins. So, the stage was set for a wonderful weekend—or not. Why? I got drunk! What the hell was I thinking?

Saturday was picture perfect. We gathered on the patio, and I (i.e., Little Barry) volunteered to bartend. Initially, I was sipping club soda and cranberry juice while everyone enjoyed their favorite cocktails and reminisced. But I was far removed from the merriment thinking about the "highs" during my drinking days. That tempting cognitive process was about to take me down the boozy slope!

Little Barry nudged me, "Come on, Barry, have one, just one. It's Thanksgiving. You have so much to be thankful for. You'll be fine." So, Little Barry caught me off guard "Go ahead; just one, it'll feel good." Rather than stave off the Machiavellian manipulations, I caved in, and moderation flew out the window! Consequently, when I served the guests, I'd knock back a double vodka. Bam! Down the hatch. My "drunk-o-meter" accelerated from feeling good to feeling better to being pissed. I awoke hours later listening to Pat chastise me for falling off the wagon.

The next morning when I awoke nursing a hangover, I was facing a shit- storm. I had managed to ruin Thanksgiving, and Pat was so upset that she was unable to prepare dinner. Fortunately, Rob and Mary stepped up to the plate. As you can imagine, the silence was deafening during the meal. I couldn't enjoy the succulent offerings, fearing I'd puke. When the guests left, Pat gave me an ultimatum, "Either you quit drinking, or I'm leaving!" My choice was obvious, and I apologized profusely. Furthermore, I promised there would never be a repeat performance.

SELF-REFLECTION

I suppose those who don't abuse alcohol will find my behaviour incomprehensible. I quit drinking in 1997, and I hadn't touched a drop since then. So, why did I fall off the wagon? Everyone was celebrating, but I wasn't feeling the joy. I wasn't feeling the way I thought I would if I got high. When Little Barry took over, "Big, Responsible, Sensible Barry" surrendered control.

EVERYTHING WAS GREAT UNTIL...

Eventually, Pat and I achieved a rapprochement of sorts and a sense of normalcy—until I received a call from my doctor in the spring of 2003. He advised that tumorous cells had been detected following a PSA test. It felt like I had been coldcocked. Seven years had passed since the operation, and now I was in another battle. So, I surfed the Internet looking for a urologist and found Dr. Joe Chin, a renowned urology-oncologist practicing in London, ON. My doctor arranged an appointment with him.

On May 13, 2003, as we drove to the hospital in London, my anxiety skyrocketed. I was concerned Dr. Chin might recommend a urologist in Owen Sound.

When we arrived at the London Health Sciences Centre, a volunteer escorted us to a waiting room overflowing with patients waiting to see Dr. Chin. This reinforced the notion that he was the best, and I wanted him on my team. However, I worried he may not be accepting new patients. I was drowning in a pool of pessimism.

When I finally met Dr. Chin, he reviewed my chart and inquired about my daily routine. I mentioned that I was a runner and had completed the Boston Marathon, which he had also run! We chatted a bit about running, and I felt our common interest might influence his decision on my becoming a patient. Wrong! Instead, he recommended a urologist in Owen Sound. "No," I blurted, "Dr. Chin, I want you to be my doctor!" After a brief pause, he acquiesced. Now that "Michael Jordan" was on my team, how could I lose?

Pat and I were chatting incessantly about Dr. Chin driving home, and I failed to notice an officer operating radar near Blyth. Busted! He admonished me for driving 20 kph over the limit. I apologized and offered no defence. The officer asked me where we were heading, and I explained that we were heading home after attending the cancer clinic at the London Health Sciences Centre. Hearing that, he returned my documents and said, "Have a safe trip, and slow down." Whew! Another good news story, and my driving record remained intact.

A couple of weeks later, the clinical coordinator of the London Regional Cancer Program called. She advised I would be billeted at the Thameswood Lodge during the six-week regime. On September 15, 2003, I arrived at the lodge and was greeted by the admittance nurse. After a brief orientation, she escorted me to my room, where I met my roommate, Ted*. He was quite friendly, and we hit it off immediately. It was comforting to share my journey with someone who could understand what I was experiencing. Ted had been diagnosed with nasal cancer, and we shared our ensuing battles. I believe folks diagnosed with cancer are akin to recovering alcoholics. They understand the struggle and are sensitive to each other's needs and concerns.

The following morning, I travelled to the cancer clinic on the lodge's minibus. Throughout the trip, I was preoccupied with uneasy thoughts about the radiation procedure. But when I arrived, my anxiety lessened somewhat when I heard a string quartet playing classical music. Also, as funny as it sounds, it was comforting to purchase a coffee from a Tim Hortons outlet. Then it was "hurry up and wait" as I sipped my coffee and watched the parade of patients passing by. Finally, I was paged.

After a brief introduction, the technicians explained that the initial session was merely a simulation. In future sessions, a radiation beam would target the cells' location. Intellectually, I understood the rationale for having a dry run on the initial visit. Nevertheless, a big part of me was disappointed that they were not trying to "kill the beast" at the earliest opportunity.

I returned to the lodge feeling somewhat conflicted. I was relieved to have learned about the treatment regime but somewhat frustrated it hadn't started yet. Following the initial week, I was having second thoughts about staying at the lodge. I wondered if the free-floating anxiety I was experiencing was triggered because I was residing with too many cancer patients. Furthermore, I detested the noisy plastic pillowcase and mattress cover on my bed. I'm a light sleeper, and the crackling sounds prevented me from enjoying a restful sleep. Unfortunately, my inability to obtain a restorative sleep and discomfort living with patients was to be my lot throughout my stay at the lodge.

LUNCH SPECIAL AND RELAPSE

I was enduring the six weeks of treatment but had far too much down time. I could still hear myself lecturing at the OPP Academy: "Anytime you are alone, bored, hungry, or emotional, you're in danger of relapsing." So, on yet another boring afternoon, I was walking by Tuffy's Tavern on Wellington Road in London when I spotted a sandwich board that said "Lunch Special: Corn Beef Sandwich with the works, $8.75. COLD BEER."

"Hey, that special looks appetizing," Little Barry whispered. "We should grab a bite to eat." So, I entered the dimly lit bar.

The odour of stale beer was unmistakable. Apropos, George Thorogood's hit song "One Bourbon, One Scotch, One Beer" was blaring in the background. I ordered a double scotch with a beer for a chaser. (Lunch could wait!) When the portly- bartender poured, I stared at the amber liquid with mouth-watering anticipation. I knocked it back, chasing it with the beer. Once again, I experienced the warm sensation as the booze trickled down my throat. Welcome back! I became a daily fixture at the bar, somewhat akin to Norm on the television series *Cheers*. I knew I was a member of the barfly club when Sam, the bartender, greeted me with, "The usual Barry?"

So, after the daily treatments I wandered through beautiful Victoria Park, a serene oasis conveniently close to the tavern, and eventually joined the barflies drinking and engaging in banter. I usually grabbed a bite to eat at around midnight and then returned to the lodge.

"Graduation day" finally arrived, and I stopped at Tuffy's to say goodbye to Sam and then headed home. The three-hour trip afforded me an opportunity to reminisce about the lodge, the treatment process, my friend Ted, and Tuffy's. *And the counterproductive decision to relapse.* I should have kicked Little Barry in the nuts! Instead, he was able to con me one more time. I needed to get back on the wagon, pronto! When I arrived home, I vowed to quit, even though I knew Little Barry was waiting to pounce. And he did!

On September 11, 2004, Jeff and Danielle were married in a lovely ceremony at the Hitching Post, a perfect setting for a wedding near Alliston, ON. Months of fretting about the weather was all for naught. When we awoke on the wedding morn, we were greeted by the ideal summer day, and the wedding was wonderful.

Following the ceremony, the guests enjoyed a delicious buffet and danced the night away. By then I had been sober for two years following my relapse in London. A few weeks prior to the wedding, I mentioned to Pat that I was going to have a couple of drinks at the wedding. Her response was predictable. "Oh, Barry, you're not going to start drinking again." I rationalized that Jeff's wedding was special, and I wanted to celebrate with a couple of drinks. Pat remained silent, realizing that arguing was futile. She probably anticipated that my "one or two" drinks would escalate to out-of-control drinking. She was right! Although I didn't get drunk at the wedding, I continued to drink afterwards, which was always a prescription for disaster.

CHAPTER 11

SNOWBIRDS

SHOVELING SNOW, SLIPPING ON SIDEWALKS, and trudging through snowbanks wasn't the life we wanted in our retirement years. So, after several trips to southwest Florida, we purchased a modest mobile home at a recreational park in Fort Myers Beach. The park is a winter haven for approximately 3,000 snowbirds. The property includes swimming pools, tennis and pickle ball courts, small lakes, and alligators. So, the sunny south became our refuge during the winter months.

BOOZE BONANZA

Florida is nirvana for alcoholics. Booze is a ubiquitous commodity that is available at convenience stores, movie theatres, service stations, sporting events, fast-food outlets, and home delivery. On our initial trip to a Publix grocery store, I was gobsmacked by the plethora of wine and beer available. When we finished shopping, we went for a drive and stopped at a Total Wine store. The outlet's inventory included over 8,000 wines, 2,500 brands of beer, and 3,000 liquors. Although the quantity and variety were impressive, the hook was the cost. Relative to Ontario, booze was cheap. For example, an Australian wine that cost $16.00 in Ontario was only $6.00 at the outlet. Suffice to say, we were frequent "flyers." (Unlike, my propensity to abuse alcohol, Pat was essentially a social drinker, who consumed alcohol in moderation.)

Cheap booze was the drawing card for me. I drank almost every day and greeted many mornings with head-crushing hangovers. However, in 2010, I reviewed our "out of country insurance" policy, which read in part, "This insurance does not cover any expenses incurred directly or indirectly as a result of the following: alcohol abuse, or an accident while being impaired by drugs or alcohol, or having an alcohol concentration that exceeds 80 milligrams in 100 milliliters of blood." Consequently, I decided to moderate my daily consumption considerably…until I didn't.

CRUISING, BOOZING, AND LOSING

In February 2012, we embarked on a South Pacific cruise with friends. Pat and I were celebrating our fortieth wedding anniversary and decided to sail in style. We departed from Honolulu, Hawaii, on *The Ocean Princess*. The vessel carried 680 passengers and 375 crew. (An ideal ratio.) The itinerary included visits to the Hawaiian Islands, Bora Bora, and Moorea, ending in Tahiti. Plenty of activities were available throughout the day, and we enjoyed poolside parties, gourmet dining, and first-class entertainment. Remarkably, I managed to control my drinking.

When we disembarked in Tahiti, we made reservations at the Intercontinental Tahiti Resort and Spa. The resort was outstanding, including acres of manicured grounds and beautiful tropical gardens. Our over-the-water bungalow (including a see-through glass floor,) was remarkable. We could see tropical fish swimming in the turquoise waters beneath us and Polynesians gliding effortlessly on their paddleboards. We decided to spend the remainder of the holiday chilling in that amazing spot.

On the final evening, our friends invited us to Le Belvedere restaurant, perched 2,000 feet up on Mont Orohena. Even though the twenty-minute drive was hair raising, it was worth it. The restaurant was in dire need of repair, but the food was delicious. The entre included beef fondue and limitless wine. We were having a wonderful evening with our friends, enjoying the sumptuous meal, but I was getting tipsy, and the over the top consumption was about to cause a shitstorm.

I was snapping pictures and noticed the sun was setting over Morea, so I took several shots. There were several, I didn't like, so I went to delete them. I was greeted by "All images will be deleted, OK?" I clicked "Yes." Then I wondered what the hell I had just done. I frantically checked the viewfinder. "Folder contains no images." Shit! All 467 "memories" were gone. I glanced around the table, and everyone was having a great time, so I kept quiet, but inside I felt miserable.

When I awoke the next morning, I wondered if I had been dreaming. Nope! So, when we gathered for breakfast, I anxiously shared the faux pas. "There's no easy way to say this. I deleted all our pictures last night." As you can imagine, my confession was greeted with silence and abject disbelief.

Surprisingly, Pat broke the ice. "It looks like I'm getting another cruise." The tentative laughter opened the door for supportive remarks.

When we returned to Fort Myers following the cruise, I visited a camera shop, hoping the pictures could be retrieved. Alas, they were gone, and I was left to lament my drunken action in a stew of guilt, disappointment, and self-recrimination.

LAST DANCE

Following the holiday and my dumb-ass stunt, I cut back on my daily intake. But an upcoming party was about to send me on another boozy "cruise!" It was being held at the park's recreation centre, and I decided to get a head start. So, I knocked back a couple of vodka shots.

Party! (Credit: Barry Ruhl)

We taxied to the party in my buddy's golf cart, and I was already feeling the blissful effects of the booze. The recreation centre was packed. The cheap booze attracted the crowd like bees to honey. We joined other party animals, and it was turning out to be a great gathering. My buddy was a wannabee waiter replenishing the beer, and I kept him busy. That's the last thing I remember.

When I regained consciousness the following morning, I was lying on our bedroom floor so drunk that I had to crawl to the bathroom. I could only recall riding to the party in the golf cart. Pat, understandably upset, filled in the blanks. She related that I was drinking like there was no tomorrow, and after far too much booze, I passed out following a dance. Our friends loaded me onto the golf cart and trucked me home. She was really pissed-off and threatened to walk unless I quit or controlled my drinking. Sheepishly, I agreed and promised her I would.

Later that day, a friend who was at the party dropped in to see how I was doing. I apologized and told him that Pat had threatened to leave. He looked me and said, "I wouldn't blame her." Ouch. That hurt, but he was right on the money.

FATHER KNOWS BEST

I had plenty of down time to consider my drunken debauchery and the effect it was having on Pat. I recalled an expression my father used. "Take a reading," he would say when he admonished me for a lacklustre effort cutting the lawn. "Fuck it," I exclaimed. He glared at me and said, "Take a reading," without elaborating. Nevertheless, I figured he wanted me to consider the inappropriate outburst. Dad didn't have a degree in psychology, but his insightful suggestion resonated when I revisited my drunken story. Why did I get drunk the night before an exam? Why did I drink so much that I required hospitalization? Why did I pick a fight with the cop in Collingwood and my supervisor? Why did I binge drink following Aunt Gladys's death? Why did I get shit-faced, after I was removed from the crime unit? And my last caper: why did I drink until I passed out at the dance? Reality check: how much longer before Pat left or I died from alcohol poisoning? In a sense, I was like Jackie Gleason, who told a reporter, "An alcoholic doesn't know why he drinks. I do. I drink to get bagged."[37]

---

37 https://drunkard.com/08_02_gleason2/

With the tragic history of alcoholism in my family, I knew I was risking my health or perhaps my life. Consequently, I promised Pat that I'd turn off the tap before getting drunk. If I didn't, I would quit. Pat was skeptical and with good reason. As Dr. Floyd P. Garrett writes in "Excuses Alcoholics Make,"

> Following an unusually painful or embarrassing episode caused by his addiction the remorseful, frequently tearful addict promises those he has harmed that nothing, absolutely nothing could ever cause him to repeat such behaviour. He may take the lead in excoriating and flagellating himself for his unpardonable sin as a demonstration of penance and a reassurance to those he has harmed or offended. Almost always effective in allaying anxiety and soothing hurt feelings on the first occasion of use, this defense rapidly loses effectiveness with repeated use as those whom it is intended to reassure become, usually with good reason, increasingly skeptical.[38]

SELF-REFLECTION

As I reflect on the loss of our memorable vacation pictures, I realize there are parallels with my alcoholism. When I review my life, I see voids where memories should exist. They were also "deleted" when I was intoxicated.

THE ENCORE

In April 2013, we returned from Florida. I was still drinking but quit before getting shitfaced. We were kept busy touring the countryside in our Corvette, fishing at Denny's Dam, working out at the fitness centre, and enjoying performances at the Stratford Festival. But then I screwed up one more time!

On August 28, 2013, we were invited to a barbecue. Prior to leaving, "Little Barry" urged me to have a double vodka. Sound familiar? There were many times I resisted his persuasions, but this time I caved. I was feeling the euphoric effects of the booze even before arriving at the party.

---

38   https://bma-wellness.com/papers/Excuses_Alcoholics.html

We noshed on burgers, and I drank copious amounts of wine. I was getting hammered! Sensible folks would have called it a night. Not me! On the way home, we stopped at another friend's house that was near our place.

A couple of hours later, and with several glasses of wine under my belt, I left feeling very intoxicated. Pat left our friend's ahead of me, and I stayed for a "nightcap." When I left, I was unable to ride my bike, so I staggered home, using the bike for support. But when I entered the lane behind our home, I crashed! For three hours I laid on the ground, helpless and scared shit-less! I was a mess. I sustained a cut to my forehead, damaged my glasses, and tore my shirt. Fortunately, I finally managed to stagger home, but as I entered the backyard, I ran into the hammock. A final crash before I hit the sack!

I awoke the next morning confronted by a concerned but unsympathetic spouse. She expressed her anger and disgust at my repeated "performance." I knew I'd hit rock bottom. "This time I'm going to quit!" I said. Pat had heard that before and was understandably skeptical.

SELF-REFLECTION

I realized that if I continued, Pat was going to leave. Hitting "bottom" opened me up to the realization that instead of fighting Little Barry, I had to accept and integrate that part of me. It meant finding ways to take care of Little Barry's needs other than turning to booze.

REDEMPTION

I quit drinking, and this time I had a vigorous resolve. Nevertheless, it was difficult. I missed the anticipation when I cracked open a bottle of wine or a chilled bottle of vodka. I endured bouts of diarrhea, night sweats, and unrelenting taunts from Little Barry to drink. I also found it particularly uncomfortable socializing because sipping a Diet Coke was not in the same league as a shot of vodka or a glass of wine. But gradually, I realized the crushing hangovers and emotional pain that Pat had endured had to go! When I was tempted to relapse, I would recall lying helplessly drunk in the lane. I was fortunate I survived. Pat reminded me that it's unbelievable I didn't die of alcohol poisoning.

SERENITY NOW

I celebrated my seventh year of sobriety on August 28, 2020. I realize I can never have another drink. The memory of crashing to the ground hopelessly drunk will always be a grim reminder that booze is my nemesis. I'm lucky to be alive and happily married to Pat and the proud patriarch of an intact family. I enjoy the simple things in life, such as toiling in our gardens, listening to our fowl friends "chatting" at the feeders, taking long walks along the Lake Huron shoreline, and treating Pat to "Ruhl's Ribs." I no longer worry where my next drink is coming from because there will be no next drink.

Together Forever (Credit: Barry Ruhl)

Barry Ruhl

BITTERSWEET GOODBYE

> Not all storms come to disrupt your life,
> some come to clear a path
>
> – *Michelle Freeman*

I devoted thirty years of my life chasing the bad guys and protecting the public. Now I'm flooded with a myriad of bittersweet memories. Three themes were intertwined during my career: the Larry Talbot investigation, CIB detective inspector, and booze.

THE LARRY TALBOT INVESTIGATION

Larry Talbot has been the focal point of my thoughts, emotions, and actions. *I still think about* him *every day*. He presented as an organized predator when he invaded our space. Organized in the sense of a well thought out plan, which could have resulted in a terrifying finality for Pat. Why? Talbot parked his vehicle at a vacant property a short distance from his cottage. I believe he was going to use the vehicle to abduct Pat. Talbot's rape kit included four sets of hockey laces and forcing Pat to raise her nightgown underscored the notion that the attack was sexually motivated. A perverse monster who acted out even with me present! The Pauline Ivy Dudley homicide in 1973 was proof positive he was capable of murder. It's unfortunate he wasn't indicted because there was a plethora of evidence. Pauline's tragic demise was the tipping point that caused me to believe he could be a serial killer, hunting for victims during his working hours He was employed by a company that had customers throughout Ontario. Was he a wolf in sheep's clothing?

When I discovered the Clinton Air Force Base was a customer, I recalled the homicide of Lynne Harper in 1959 and the conviction of Steven Truscott for her homicide. Did the OPP arrest the wrong person? Did Larry Talbot kill Lynne Harper? That surreal hypothesis was an upsetting question for the OPP because it essentially meant Truscott may have been wrongfully convicted.

On September 22, 2000, *thirty months* after the OPP received my report, Talbot was interviewed at his residence. It began at 12:25 and concluded at 13:04. They asked him thirteen questions. He was also asked to take a polygraph examination, and he agreed. The examination was never done.

On July 1, 2008, forty years after the cottage invasion, Talbot called us, supposedly to apologize to Pat. Ironically, that call caused the OPP to initiate an investigation. However, he died on September 8, 2008, six days before he was going to be interviewed by the CIB. Many unanswered questions died with him. The Teflon monster should have been investigated when the OPP received my initial report in 1997. Why wasn't it done?

CIB DETECTIVE INSPECTOR

After a few years of criminal investigations, the brass realized I was effective chasing bad guys. Consequently, I was assigned to the District 6 Criminal Investigation Squad (CIS) and selected to be the district intelligence coordinator. I had my sights set on becoming a CIB detective inspector. I thought that dream would become a reality when I was transferred to the crime unit at Barrie district headquarters. However, when I was removed from the unit, the dream became a nightmare! After I retired, Pat suggested I opened a can of worms when I chased Larry Talbot for the Lynne Harper homicide. I suspect that was the straw that broke the camel's back. Nevertheless, I began a second and rewarding career as an addiction counsellor, and for that I am grateful to the OPP.

BOOZE

This book is called *Booze and the Badge* because I had an on-again, off-again relationship with alcohol. I wonder how many readers will be shocked by the boozy episodes. When I was discussing the book with a dear friend, he said, "I can't believe you didn't get into shit, lose your job, your health, or Pat!" He was right! I played fast and loose with my nemesis, and I survived. But I also served the public for thirty years and was the OPP addiction counsellor. And to a large extent, booze never interfered with those roles. Yes, there were occasions when I was tempted to call in sick when hungover, but I never did. Fortunately, the Donwood and some dear friends were my saving grace. While there have been hiccups along the winding road, I'm celebrating seven years of sobriety, and it feels good.

Yesterday is history, tomorrow's a mystery, and today is a gift.[39]

God grant me the serenity to accept the things I cannot change,
the courage to change the things I can,
and the wisdom to know the difference.

– Reinhold Niebuhr (1892–1971)

---

39 http://cleanandsobernotdead.com/Meeting%20Quotes/Meeting%20Quotes.html

EPILOGUE
A WIFE'S PERSPECTIVE

AS BARRY HAS SHARED THROUGHOUT his story, living with an alcoholic spouse struggling with their addiction brings with it a constant roller-coaster of emotions: fear of what behaviors the drinking will bring about, fear of a relapse in sobriety, fear of the impact on our child, resentment for staying, resentment for neglecting my own feelings, and the guilt, shame, and pain produced by a continuous narrative of self-doubt and second-guessing. Over our nearly fifty-year journey together, I experienced all these feelings at different times and often simultaneously. I experienced them while he was drinking, and I experienced them during his sobriety. There were times when I was prepared to throw in the towel, but I told myself he would get better, that things would work out in time. Many times, they did, and sometimes they did not.

While addiction will always remain a feature of our relationship, our life has not been exclusively impacted by alcohol, and we have shared many joys, accomplishments, and intimacies throughout our marriage—and continue to do so! In this regard, I am fortunate. Many spouses of addicts do not share this connection. I am proud of Barry for having the strength to continue fighting his addiction and to share his story here. Today I can finally say I am proud of myself for having the strength and resilience to persevere even when I felt I was at the rock bottom of our relationship and struggling to make the right decisions for myself and my family.

Spouses are often held captive in the passenger seat of their partner's addiction. This is especially compounded when you are in a relationship with a member of the police or another first responder. Too often we suffer in silence as work-related PTSD and negative coping mechanisms (e.g. addiction, domestic abuse, emotional abuse) become internalized and normalized in the home. Over much of Barry's career, there were no supports in place for spouses and partners. I wish there were. If I can share any advice, if you are in a relationship fraught with addiction or abuse, please reach out and find support. You are not alone! If you need help, Al-Anon (www.al-anon.org) is a mutual support organization for the families and friends of alcoholics.

CPSIA information can be obtained
at www.ICGtesting.com
Printed in the USA
BVHW021934060321
601532BV00010B/1